The Country Schools of Ogemaw County: Volume One

Ogemaw County Country Schools
Althea Cascadden Phillips. Copyright © 2016.
ISBN 0692696-5. Library of Congress

Ogemaw County Genealogical & Historical Society

Other Publications Available From:

Ogemaw County Genealogical & Historical Society

First Landowners of Ogemaw County

Ogemaw County Historical Review

The History of Oriolette Basketball

6 Unique Driving Tour Booklets

Ogemaw County
Genealogical & Historical Society
Presents

The Country Schools of Ogemaw County

Volume 1

2nd Edition

Researched and Compiled by
Althea Cascadden Philips
First Volume in a Series

To submit additions or corrections, please contact
The Ogemaw Society at
Post Office Box 734
West Branch, MI 48661

FORWORD

This book covers the first seventeen of the Ogemaw County Country Schools, in alphabetical order. Some schools have had more than one name, and others have been moved to different locations during their years of use. For many, there is a lot of information. For some, especially the very early ones, there is little.

The foundation for this book was taken from the research of Ada Fritz and Genevieve Bemis. They gathered pages and pages of names and dates which supplied a wonderful starting point. Much information was supplied to them by students and teachers and some was not completely accurate, but again it was a beginning.

Many scrapbooks contained bits of information; interviews with teachers and students added their memories of school life and names of fellow attendees; newspaper articles and school pictures added a bit more and slowly this book about our country schools began to develop.

Proper spelling of names or identification of pictures has been difficult and errors undoubtedly exist. Apologies are made for these errors and it is hoped that corrections can be made in reprints of this material in the future.

DEDICATION

This book is dedicated to all the teachers who spent so many hours for so little pay, so that we could become educated. It is also dedicated to members of my family who taught and went to these country schools.

ACKNOWLEDGEMENTS

Special thanks go to Ada Fritz and Geneveive Bemis who asked the questions and left us the answers so we could remember all the teachers and students that went before us.

Thank you to all the people who gave us pictures to use and stories to print in this book.

Special thank you goes to Sally Rea, Lois Bergquist, and LuAnn Zettle who have assisted me during hours of research and answered all my questions.

Thank you to Grace Dooley and Judy Bedtelyon who provided pictures from the notebooks at the Withey School located at the Ogemaw County Fairgrounds. Special thanks to the Rose City Area Historical Society for the use of the photographs in their collection. A special thank you to Mercy Huizar who donated many hours of her time to make this volume possible.

COUNTRY SCHOOLS

(Author Unknown)

The auctioneer's chant brings an ache to my heart, as the old country school has to go,
For old country schools are a thing of the past, but it's part of my childhood, you know.
The little brass bell we dreaded to hear, as it called the children from play,
Will bring a good price as the auctioneer chants, for it is an antique today.

The old desk with initials carved in the top, by some school boy not minding his book,
Or perhaps he was dipping pigtails in the ink, real quick, before teacher could look.
The lunch pails all sit on a bench by the door, grape basket, syrup pail made of tin,
But the bright red tin box, the prize of them all, that Grandad's tobacco came in.

Homemade bread and jelly was standard fare then, an apple and a cookie we got,
And nobody worried it would ruin our health because the noon meal wasn't hot.
Germs were not discussed in those long ago days, the water pail had one dipper for all,
The old coal burning stove, with its smoke and its dirt when chilly days came in the fall.

The games that we played, "pump, pump pull away," or "hide and seek" always were found,
Or perhaps fox and geese when the weather was cold, and snow had covered the ground.
The two little houses that set back always, with words on the door "Girls" and "Boys,"
Many a secret was whispered inside as we shared all our sorrows and joys.

The bright sunny locks of the boys and girls then, now have all turned to gray,
And many have answered that final roll call, but I see them in memory today.
The old must give way to the new, it is true, and that is the way it must be,
But that old country school, tho' a thing of the past, holds many fond memories for me.

TABLE OF CONTENTS

Atherton School 1
Beaver Lake School 31
Beechwood School 32
Bell School 35
Busenbark School 43
Bush Lake School 49
Campbell Corners School 51
Caverly School 69
Cook School 71
Cranberry Lake School 89
Dale School 95
Damon School 105
Deckerville School 109
East Side School 111
Edwards School 137
Erb School 157
Evergreen School 183
General Information vii
Index xxi

SCHOOL LOCATIONS
OGEMAW COUNTY TOWNSHIPS

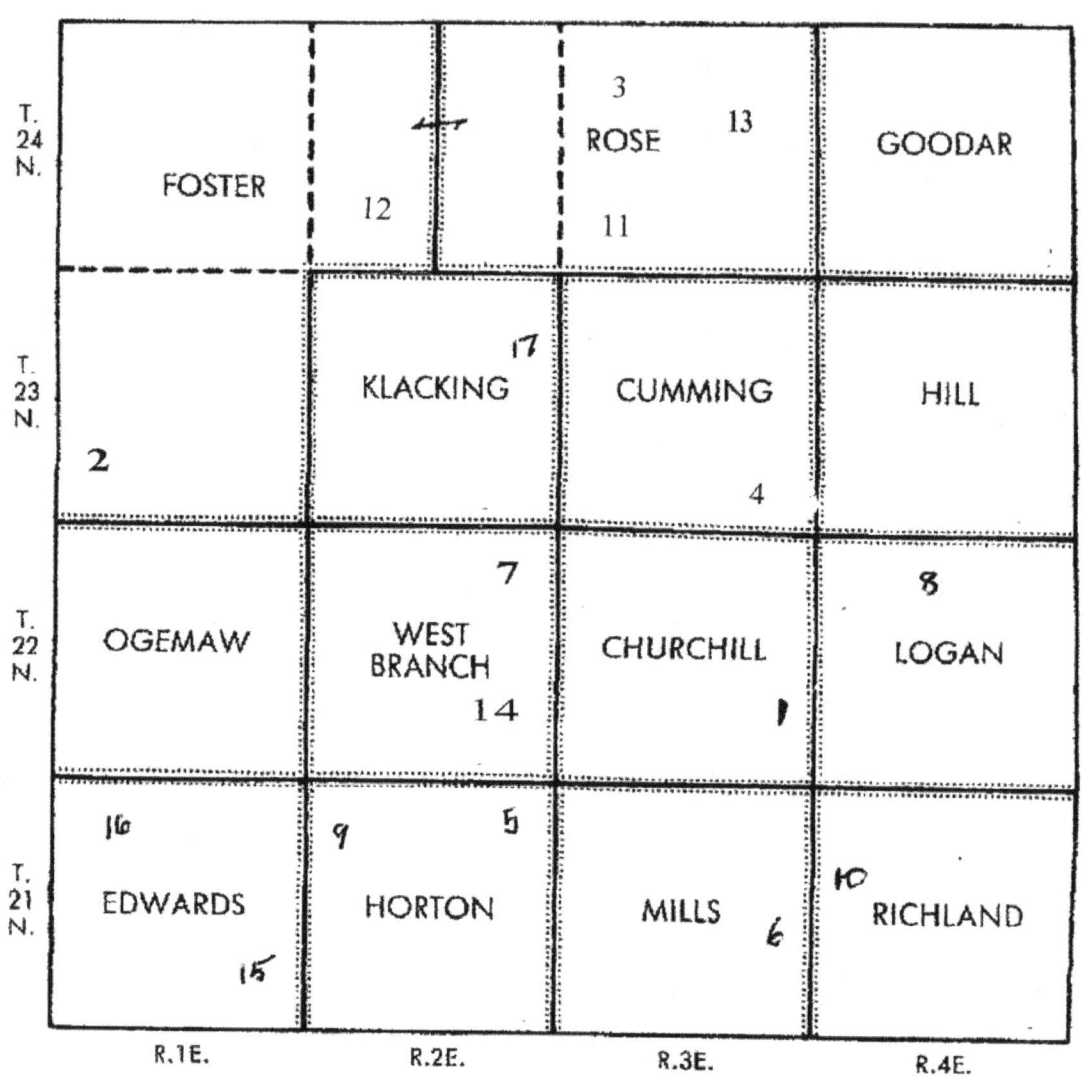

1. Atherton
2. Beaver Lake
3. Beechwood
4. Bell
5. Busenbark
6. Bush Lake
7. Campbell Corners
8. Caverly
9. Cook
10. Cranberry Lake
11. Dale
12. Damon
13. Deckerville
14. Eastside
15. Edwards
16. Erb
17. Evergreen

The Country Schools of Ogemaw County: Volume 1

ATHERTON SCHOOL

Churchill Township (Town 22 North Range 3 East)

NE ¼ of NE ¼ of Section 25, Henderson Lake Road at M-55

Ogemaw County Genealogical & Historical Society

ATHERTON SCHOOL

Churchill Township (Town 22 North Range 3 East)

NE ¼ of NE ¼ of Section 25, Henderson Lake Road at M-55

Teachers:

1910-1911 Harrison Dodds; 1912 Susie Richardson; 1923-1924 Ansel Abbott; 1924 Mr. Abbott; 1925 Lavina Jones; 1926-1927 Helen David; 1927-1928 Clarence Cooley; 1930-1932 Arzell Walker Williams; 1932-1933 Eugenie Rice McDonald; 1934-1935 Harry Kenyon; 1935-1939 Mona Mills; 1940-1941 Donald DeMatio (killed in war); 1947-1949 Margaret Freeborn Howe; 1949-1950 Eleanor Derenick; 1950's Dennis Clark; 1950-1951 Lorene Rakestraw; 1952-1954 Wilma Quigley; 1954-1956 Virginia Simmons; 1957-1958 Virginia Simmons Clark; 1958-1961 Rosella Polmanteer Dennis; 1961-1964 Helen Sturtevant Unknown dates: Minnie Bennett Dodds, Wenona Gibson Netzlaff, Grace Dodds Switzer, Ada Quigley Norris, Electa Withey, Dora Boddy, Florine Turner, Anna Walker Heath

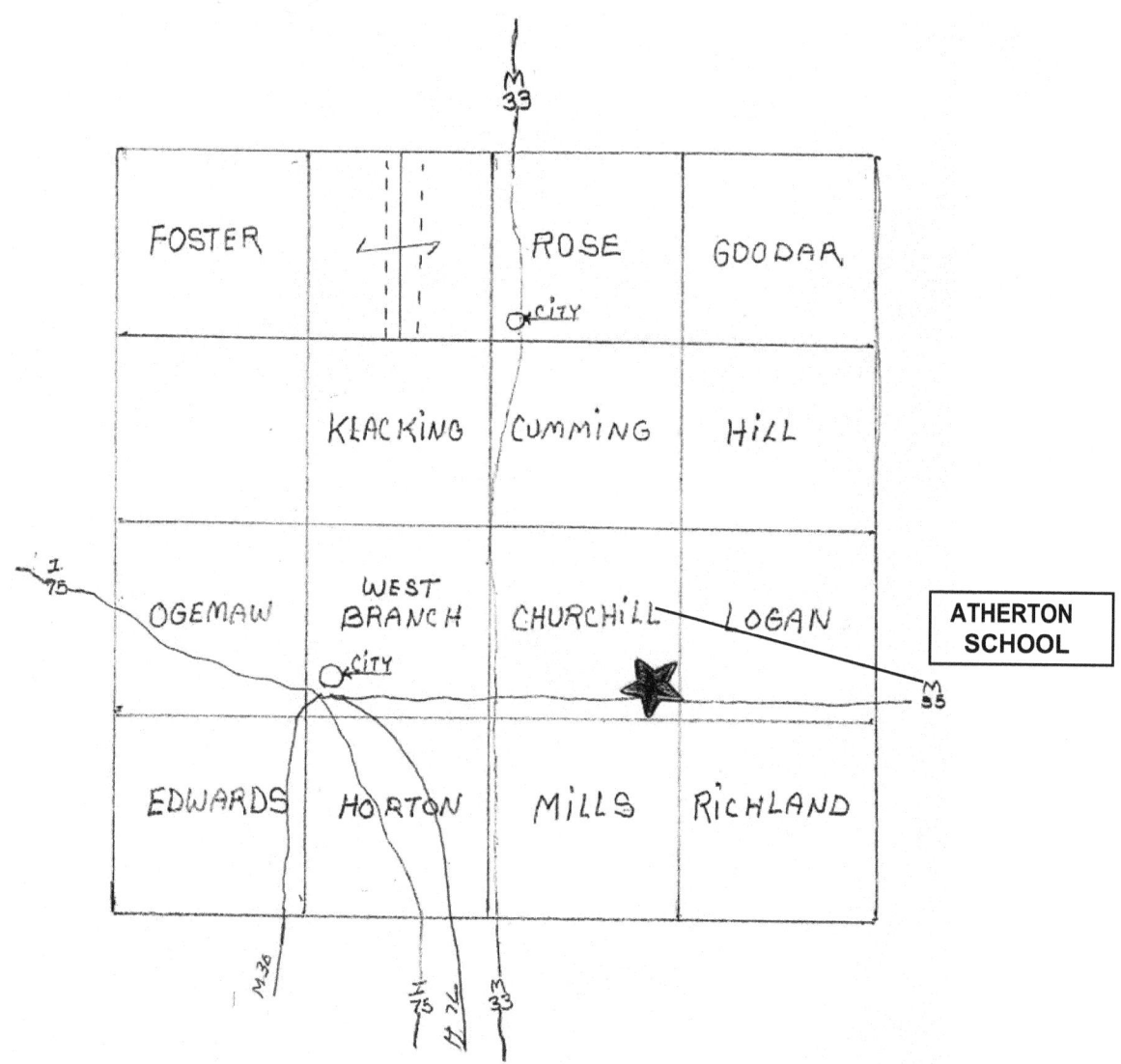

ATHERTON SCHOOL

Churchill Township (Town 22 North Range 3 East)

NE ¼ of NE ¼ of Section 25, Henderson Lake Road at M-55

Students:

Allen: Myrtle, Ralph; **Atherton:** Willard, Thelda, Oren; **Baldwin:** Ruth; **Barnum:** Mildred, Robert, Stella, John, Harold; **Bauman:** Harold; **Belanger:** Louise, Emelda, Corrine, Arthur, Delamae, Velma, Jack; **Best:** Flora; **Bowman:** Ola, Earl, Ray, Mary Sue, Ralph, Mable; **Copeland:** Florene, Duane, Charlotte; **Curry:** Margaret, Donley; **David:** Dewey, Helen, Bernice, Mae, Janice, Chester, Byron, Daniel, Doyle, Louis, Arthur, Velma, DellaMae; **Dodds:** Grace, Gladys, Elmer, Mable, Eugene, Harrison, Marion, Thelma; **Eastman:** George, Iva, Neva, Eva, Raymond, Frances, Leon, Howard, Jack, Betty, Sally; **Goatbe:** Georgia, Norma, Arthur **Good**: Sally, Wilbur, Orville, Orland, Mildred, Ada, Nancy, Barbara, Leroy, Rosemary, Henry, Sonny, Billy, Bobby, Geraldine, Geneane; **Holshoe:** Noreen, Dick, Agnes, IvaDell, Frank, Jerry, Alice, Donald, Victor; **Hook:** Carleen, Renal; **Horning:** Raymond, Ruth, Marjorie, Leighton, Lotamae; **Hostetler:** Ezra; **Houck:** Earl, Ezra, Marcia, Carolyn, Edward, Hazel; **Joye:** Jerry, Judy; **Leckrone:** Samuel; **Martindale:** Ilene, Alice, Aliene, Viola, Tom, Esther; **Mason:** Mable, Fern, Harold, Wendel, Steve, Sally, Bonnie, Donna, Twila; **Mier:** Harvey, Rosemary, Tom, Mike, Paul; **Meiser:** David, Glen; **Mier:** Victor, Ralph; **Migan:** Helen; **Miller:** Douglass, Norman, Beverly, Raymond; **Moats:** Vera, Lois, Florence, Edith, Zeta, Hazel; **Morehouse:** Ronald, Kenneth, Brenda, Eddie, Richard, Nancy, Millie; **Myers:** Jennie, Lena, Helen, Pearl, Marcella; **Norris:** Arlene, Kenneth, Alla, Jennie, Lila, Ora, Leona, Devere, Donley, Maynard, Dennis; **Olson:** Viola, Gladys, Eva, Ethel; **Payne:** Elmer, George, Hazel, Mae, Alma; **Peterson:** Rissie, Blaine, Mary Ann, Emerson, Eldin, Beatrice, Henry, Floyd, Pearl, Willard, Linda; **Robinson:** Kathleen; **Rowe:** Dean, Joyce; **Ryan:** Mickey; **Snooks:** Myrtle, Viola, Mary Jane, Johnny; **Stone:** Robert, Leah, Eva, Mary, Bonnie, Christina, Harold; **Switzer:** Dorothy, Berdie, Charlie, Dean, Harold; **Thorn:** Mary Ann, Nelson; **Thorne:** Alfred, William, Viola; **Trout:** Marvin, Erma, Rita, Beverly, Verah; **VanWormer:** Lucille; **Wyman:** Hattie, Elaine

ATHERTON SCHOOL

There were four 4-H clubs: Handicraft, Electrical, Sewing, and Baking Clubs. These were organized in the 1950's and were very popular.

A memorable Christmas program for Betty Eastman was the year two of the boys, Jack Belanger and Nelson Thorn had to dress up as girls. She also remembers how much she liked the dances in the spring music festival.

Mrs. Dennis was Mary Ann Peterson's teacher, and she had also been her mother's teacher in Saginaw. Since the Peterson children lived a long way from the school, Mrs. Dennis would pick them up on her way. The three Peterson's liked the ride, they would remain after school and do the cleaning, to get a ride home. Needless to say, they were considered the "Teacher's Pet".

Norma Goatbe seemed to find herself getting into mischief quite often. Once her teacher made her go outside and walk around the school backwards a number of times.

One day in January, 1924, Mr. Abbott was conveyed to his school by sled.

Donald DeMatio, after teaching in the Atherton school, graduated as an Air Force Pilot on December 5, 1943. He was killed in action in Europe in July of 1944.

Atherton School was closed for most of a week due to the death of the teacher's (Ansel Abbott) grandmother.

ATHERTON SCHOOL
Harrison Dodds, Teacher
1910-1911

Top Row:
Rissie Peterson, Jennie Myers, Grace Dodds, Gladys Dodds, Ola Bowman, Lena Myers, Helen Myers, Harrison Dodds (teacher), Earl Bowman Hattie Wyman, Myrtle Snooks, Pearl Myers, Elmer Dodds, Blaine Peterson, Dewey David, George Eastman, Wendel Mason, Mable Dodds, Mabel Mason, Lila Norris, Viola Snooks, Ralph Bowman, Steve Mason.

Ogemaw County Genealogical & Historical Society

ATHERTON SCHOOL

Top Row:

1912

Earl Bowman, Dewey David, Iva Eastman, Mary Sue Bowman, Susie Richardson (teacher), Rissie Peterson, Myrtle Allen, Ralph Allen.

Middle Row:

Hattie Wyman, Fern Mason, Mabel Mason, Lila Norris, Mable Dodds, Neva Eastman, Jennie Norris, Myrtle Snooks, Viola Snooks, Mary Jane Snooks.

Front Row:

Elmer Dodds, George Eastman, Steve Mason, Wendel Mason, Blaine Peterson, Ralph Bowman, Johnny Snooks, Ezra Hostetler, unknown Richey, unknown

The Country Schools of Ogemaw County: Volume 1
ATHERTON SCHOOL

Steve Mason, Elmer Dodds, George Eastman, Tom Martindale, Leander unknown, Leona unknown, Viola Olson, Hazel Payne, Gladys Olson, Minnie Bennett Dodds (teacher), Marcella Myers, Mae Payne, Alma Payne, Helen Myers, Esther Martindale, unknown, Richie, Earl Houck, Ralph Bowman, Elmer Payne, George Payne, Ezra Hostetler, Alla Norris, Mable Dodds, Eva Olson, Neva Eastman, Hattie Wyman, Hazel Moats, Pearl Myers, Vera Moats, Kenneth Norris, Lila Norris, Helen David, Mable Mason, Ethel Olson, Ilene Martindale, Jennie Norris, Alice Martindale, Florence Moats, unknown Weiwork, unknown Weiwork, Louise Belanger, Mable Bowman, Ora Norris, unknown Olson, Berdie Switzer.

ATHERTON SCHOOL

Persons in this picture but not in order:

*Fern Mason, Vera Moats,
Alice Martindale,
Aliene Martindale,
Lois Moats,
Raymond Horning,
Berdie Switzer,
Florence Moats,
Alla Norris, Jennie Norris,
Edith Moats, Wilbur Good,
Orville Good, Orland Good,
Harold Mason,
Ruth Horning,
Viola Martindale,
Helen Migan,
Mildred Good,
Marjorie Horning,
Charlie Switzer, Zeta Moats.
Ansel Abbot, teacher*

In picture:

*Louise Belanger,
Alice Martindale,
Aliene Martindale,
Elmer Payne, George Payne,
Emelda Belanger,
Corrine Belanger,
Edith Moats,
Raymond Horning,
Ruth Horning,
Marjorie Horning, Erma
unknown Florence Moats,
Hazel unknown, Wilbur
Good.*

ATHERTON SCHOOL

ATHERTON SCHOOL

Background:
Ada Good
Back Row:
Aliene Martindale, Charlie Switzer, George Payne, Alice Martindale
Front Row:
Louise Belanger, Neva Eastman, Jennie Norris

ATHERTON SCHOOL
Eighth Grade Graduation

Leona Norris, Raymond Eastman, Wilbur Good, Emelda Belanger, and Lucille VanWormer.

ATHERTON SCHOOL
1931

Row 1:

Willard Atherton, Howard Eastman, Dewey David, Edward Houck, Arzell Walker (teacher), Marion Dodds, Elaine Wyman, Dorothy Switzer, Lila Norris, Velma David

Row 2:

Byron David, Frank Holshoe, Maynard Norris, Harold Bauman, Leighton Horning, Thelda Atherton, Hazel Houck, Thelma Dodds, Ivadell Holshoe, DellaMae David

Row 3:

Arthur David, Chester David, Donley Norris, William Thorne, Dean Rowe, Oren Atherton, Emerson Peterson, Mae David, Agnes Holshoe, Lotamae Horning, Joyce Rowe, Arlene Norris, Viola Thorne

ATHERTON SCHOOL

OGEMAW COUNTY HERALD
January 28, 1937

ATHERTON SCHOOL GETS ELECTRICITY
First Rural School in County to Get Lights

The Atherton school in Churchill Township is the first rural school in Ogemaw County to have electric lights, according to Miss Delia B. Neal, county school commissioner.

The school board comprised of J.F. Atherton, A. Dodds, and A. J. Norris, have proposed this improvement as a measure to make their school as modern as possible. There is a line running nearby that several farmers of the vicinity have been connected with for some time. It is believed that the expense will be very reason- able under the new rural electrification program.

Miss Mona Mills of Prescott is the teacher of the school.

ATHERTON SCHOOL
1948

Persons included in this picture:

Billy Good, Bobby Good, Goatbe girls, Jack Belanger, Florene Copeland, Alfred Thorne, Stella Barnum, Sonny Good, Geraldine Good, Norene Holshoe, Geneane Good, Mildred Barnum, Nancy Good, Barbara Good.

The Country Schools of Ogemaw County: Volume 1

ATHERTON SCHOOL

1952 - 1953 Calendar

September

    2 - School opened with 33 percent

    8 - Frank Holshoe came to school

    11 - Get Acquainted Party for the Mothers

October

    7 - First Mother's Club meeting

    21 - Eva Stone left to live in Bay Co.

    31 - Halloween Party

November

    3 - Samuel Leckrone came to our school - Brethren, Mich.

    21 - Movies, pie, and ice cream

December

    23 - Christmas Program

February

    14 - Valentine Party

    27 - Movies and auction sale at Logan Hall

March

    2 - Eva Stone returned to our school

    19 - Linda Peterson came to us from Pontiac

April

    16 - Ball game at Palmer School (there) Remember the score

    25 - Movies, quilt raffle, pie, and ice cream for the 6th, 7th, and 8th grades

    30 - Music Festival

May

    2 - Achievement Day

    18 - Ball game with Palmer School (here)

    22 - Picnic

    26 - Report card day

RURAL SCHOOL MUSIC FESTIVAL
West Branch High School Gymnasium
April 30, 1953 8:00 p.m.

Wanda Virginia Cook, Director

Ruth Basham, Accompanist

Entire Chorus -
For the Beauty of the Earth
Pledge to the Flag
The Star Spangled Banner

Lower Grades -
One, Two Buckle My Shoe
The Wake-Up Clock
See That Elephant
Eency, Weency Spider

Upper Grades -
Rhythmical Rain
Spring Morning

Lower Grades -
Come, My Ponies
I Want to Sail
The Bus

Folk Games -
Bluebird Through My Window
Klapp Dans

Upper Grades -
Big Corral
Go 'Way Old Man
Wait, Old Mule
Goin' to Shout

Lower Grades -
If I Could
Things I Like Best
Its Spring

Folk Games -
Brown-Eyed Mary
The Hatter

Upper Grades -
The Indian Flute
Hawaii
In the Plaza

Finale -
Now the Day is Over

ATHERTON SCHOOL

4-H HANDICRAFT CLUB

Seven boys started their Handicraft Club in November, 1952. Mr. Barnum was their leader. After Christmas Mr. Barnum was unable to continue as a leader. Ollie Coon helped the boys for a few weeks, and then he moved away. Russell Baldwin consented to help the boys finish their work.

Norman Miller and Samuel Leckrone were the first year members. They each made a sanding block, a what-not-shelf, and a bread box. Norman made a milk stool and a feed scoop. Sam made a pair of door stops and a broom holder.

Donald Holshoe and John Barnum were the second year members. Don made a laundry cart, sleeve board, spice shelf, and a foot stool. John made two what-not-shelves, a kitchen shelf, and a sleeve board.

Marvin Trout, doing third year work, made a clothes hamper, cedar chest, and waste basket.

Raymond Miller, in his fourth year of work made a desk and a tool chest.

Marvin and Donald received the red ribbons and the other boys the blue

ribbons.

4-H ELECTRICAL CLUB

The Atherton 4-H boys began their electrical project in January, 1953, under the supervision of Russell Baldwin.

First year boys were Sam Leckrone and Norman Miller. They assembled extension cords, and repaired appliance cords. Norman made an electric clock time switch. Sam made a movable spot light.

Raymond Miller, third year member, converted an ice cream freezer into a power unit, and wired the family garage.

Sam brought home a red ribbon and the other two boys received blue ribbons.

ATHERTON SCHOOL
WHO'S WHO

Victor Mier - is new to our neighborhood

Bonnie Stone - the quiet second grader

Frank Holshoe - started the measle epidemic

Dennis Norris - had chicken-pox instead of measles

Eugene Dodds - takes a long time to get home from school

Marcia Houck - is always reading

Beverly Trout - the dark haired girl

Rosemary Good - our little warbler

Arthur Goatbe - never cries, even when he gets hurt

Jerry Joye - is the boy with the smile

Jerry Holshoe - thinks school is hard work

Sally Mason - is our bashful blonde

Ralph Mier - is going to be a "six footer"

Mary Ann Peterson - likes to write on the blackboard

Douglass Miller - the youngest of the "Miller boys"

Linda Peterson - came to us from Pontiac

Christina Stone - Verah Trout - and Eldin Peterson are the three beginners who had a hard time to learn to sit still

ATHERTON SCHOOL
1953

ATHERTON SCHOOL
1953

The Country Schools of Ogemaw County: Volume 1

ATHERTON SCHOOL
1953

Ogemaw County Genealogical & Historical Society

ATHERTON SCHOOL
1953

Fifth

Marvin Trout
John Barnum
Eva Stone
Judy Joye
Mary Ann Thorn
Robert Stone
Norman Miller
Donald Holshoe
Mo Erma Trout

ATHERTON SCHOOL
1953

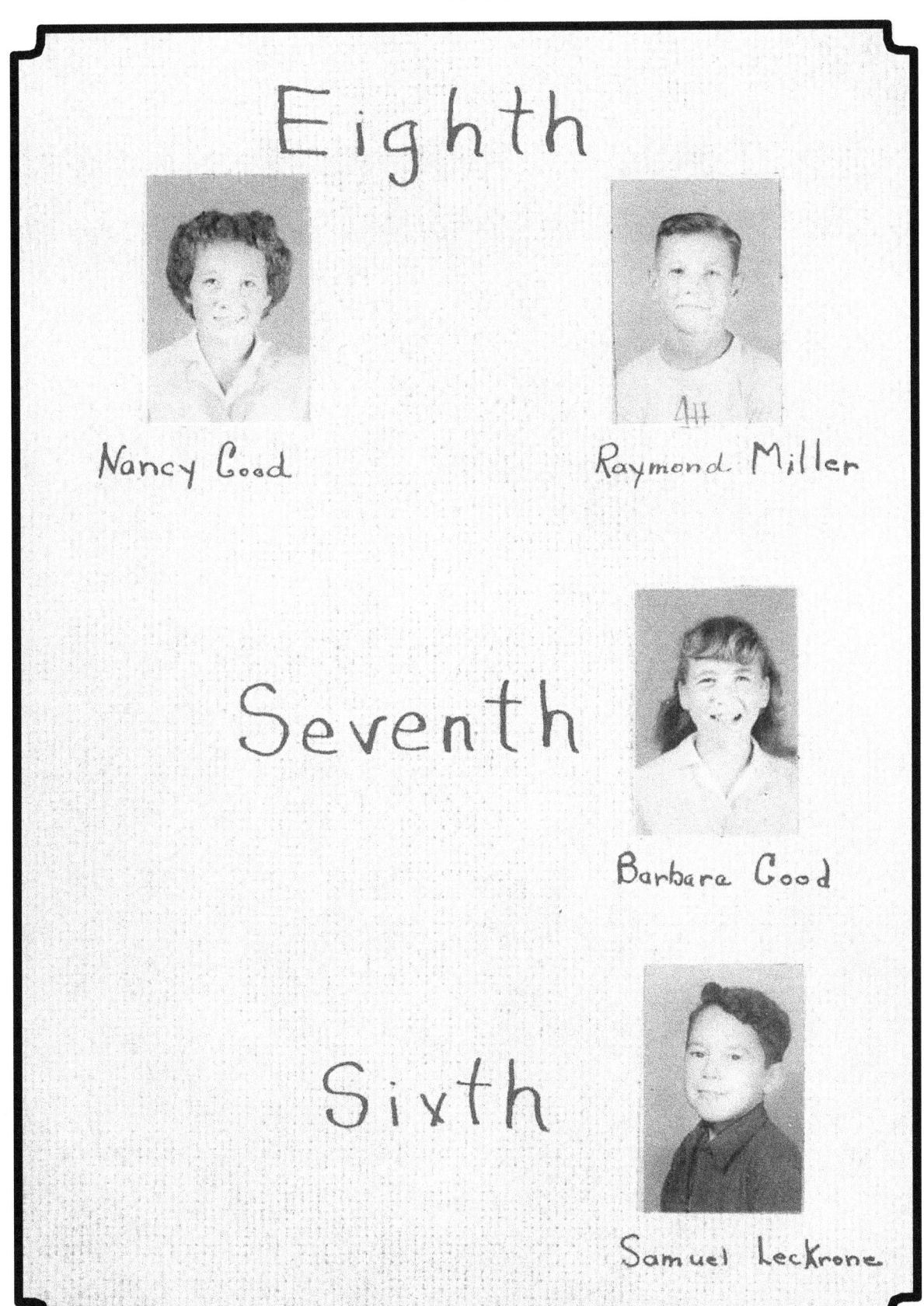

ATHERTON SCHOOL
1953

Raymond and his 4H desk.

The 4 H'ers

The Klapp Dans Trio

Sewing Girls

ATHERTON SCHOOL
1953

Teacher 1952-1953 Wilma Quigley

Strike One! Nancy and Raymond

Atherton School

Rev. and Mrs. Leckrone "Our Chapel Leaders"

Ogemaw County Genealogical & Historical Society

ATHERTON SCHOOL
1958

The Country Schools of Ogemaw County: Volume 1

ATHERTON SCHOOL

Back row:

Sally Good, Rosella Dennis (teacher), Bonnie Stone, Sally Mason, Mary Ann Peterson.

Front row:

Jerry Joye, Jerry Holshoe, Douglass Miller, Frank Holshoe, Ralph Mier.

Nelson Thorn, Mickey Ryan, Noreen Holshoe, Geraldine Good, Bernice David, Jack Belanger.

ATHERTON SCHOOL

ATHERTON SCHOOL
Eighth Grade Trip

Back Row:

Douglass Miller, Bonnie Stone, Mary Ann Peterson, Rosella Dennis (teacher), Jerry Holshoe, Frank Holshoe, Ralph Mier.

Front Row:

Sally Mason, Sally Good

ATHERTON SCHOOL
Eighth Grade Trip

Bay City Park, Eighth grade graduation.

Sonny Good, Florene Copeland, Duane Copeland

BEAVER LAKE SCHOOL

Foster Township (Town 23 North Range 1 East and west half of Town 24 North Range 2 East)

NE 1/4 of NE 1/4 of Section 31 Gone by 1928

Teacher:

1923-1924 Grace Plancher (new school)

Students:

Miss Grace Plancher of West Branch has been appointed to teach at Beaver Lake School for the school year 1923-24.

BEECHWOOD SCHOOL

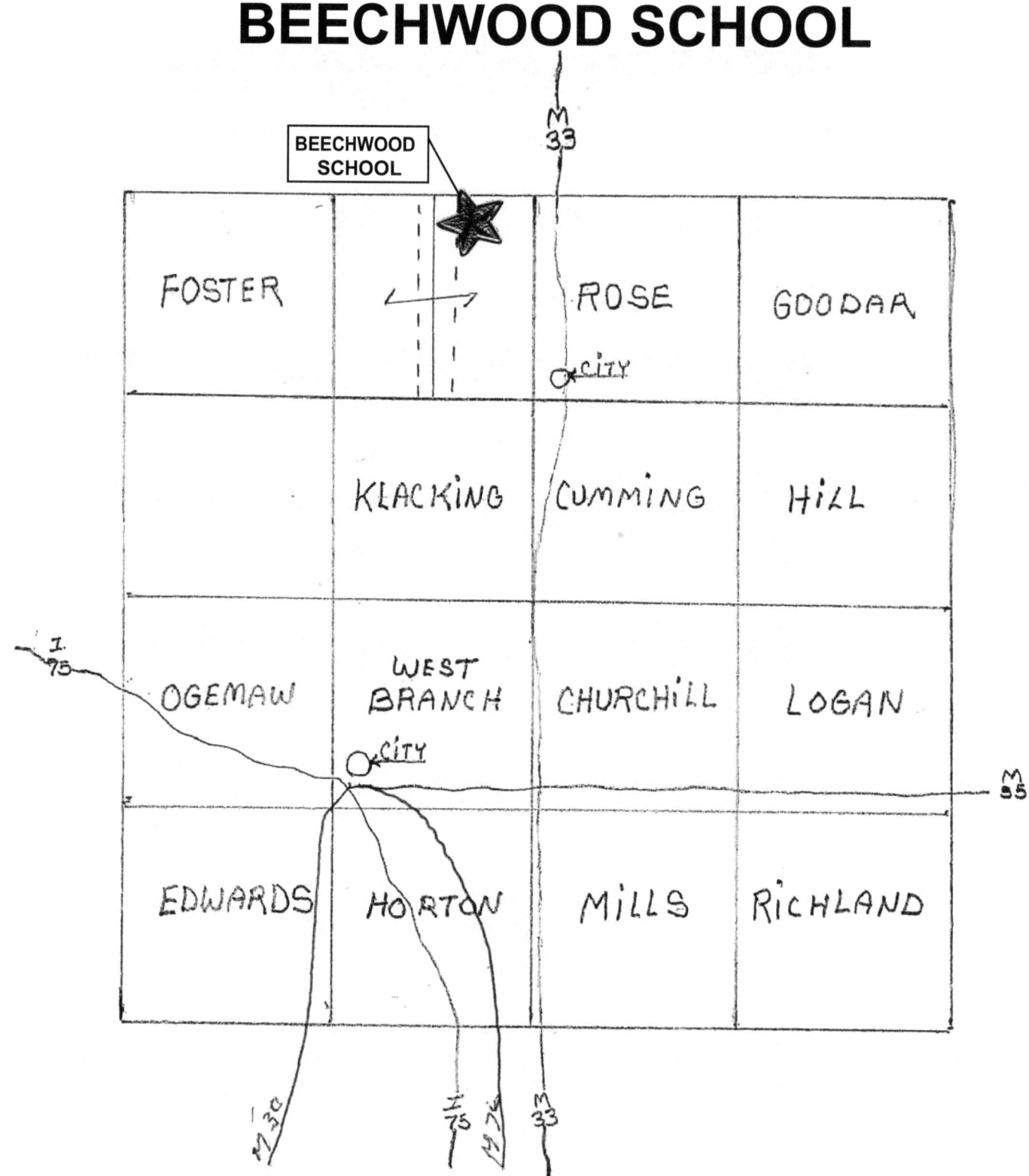

BEECHWOOD SCHOOL

Rose Township (Town 24 North Range 2 East [west half] and Town 24 North Range 3 East)

NW ¼ of NE ¼ of Section 8

BEECHWOOD SCHOOL

Rose Township (Town 24 North Range 2 East [west half] and Town 24 North Range 3 East)

NW ¼ of NE ¼ of Section 8

Teachers:

1927-1928 Theresa Harcourt Slater; 1929-1930 Gladys Ide; 1930-1934 Gertrude Butler Marx; 1932-1933 Irma Mier; 1933-1934 Mary Smith Burgess; 1935-1936 Joseph DeMatio; 1936 Helen David Migan; 1936-1937 William Fuhrman; 1937 Miss Kuhn; 1937-1939 Ethel Mayhew; 1939-1941 Virginia Martin; 1946-1949 Bertina DeKett Graber

Students:

Barber: Jack, Mervin, Thelma; **Daniels:** Geraldine; **Inman:** George, Hazel, Leon, Neil; **Mayhew:** Cherrian, Wayne, Betty; **Nelson:** Lewis, Seymour; **Sheldon:** Ellen, Forest; **Teeples:** Ellis, Lewis, JR, Lawrence, Lavern

In 1937, a visiting nurse came to give physical examinations, along with shots. It was decided that several students needed to have their tonsils out, much to the dismay of the students.

BEECHWOOD SCHOOL NEWS

1937

MISS KUHN, Teacher

Dr. Sue Thompson and Miss Manilla Campbell, our nurse, visited our school on Tuesday and we were glad to get our physical examinations and protection against diphtheria and smallpox. A number of us need to have our tonsils out. We appreciate the work of our medical department. We wish to thank our school for the new lavatories, cloakroom, sink, and water fountain. We find that these have greatly improved our school environment. Those who were neither absent nor tardy this month are: Mervin Barber, Leon Inman, Hazel Inman, George Inman, Betty Mayhew, Ellen Sheldon, and Forest Sheldon. This is a good start, we hope to add more to our list next month. A number of us have improved a great deal on our Penmanship while a few of us need more practice. We are planning to make Portfolios for art class, until our material comes.

BELL SCHOOL

Cumming Township (Town 23 North Range 3 East)

NW ¼ of SW ¼ of Section 36 on Pettit Road

Opened 1915, closed October 1944

BELL SCHOOL

Cumming Township (Town 23 North Range 3 East)

NW ¼ of SW ¼ of Section 36 on Pettit Road

Opened 1915, closed October 1944

Teachers:

1900 Flora Scheele Rau; 1927-1930 Anna Walker Heath; 1931-1932 Mrs. Kenyon; 1934-1936 Rosella Dennis; 1935 Ethel Mayhew; 1941-1942 Cameron Sutton; 1944-1945 Floy Thompson; 1953 Miss Kuhn <u>Unknown dates</u>: Mae LaDue (when it was a log cabin), Harry Kenyon, Marian Kenyon, Maud Kenyon, Irene Miller McCoy, Bernetta Finerty Goodrich, Electa Withey Winegar, Maud Embury, Jennie Cook, Grace Switzer, Lanora Markell, Helen David Migan, Rosella Polmanteer

Students:

Brown: Laura; **Cornell:** Patricia, Leon, Mervin; **Davis:** Warren; **Duvekott:** Edna; **Fritz:** Stephen, Lillian, Joan, Mina, John; **Hall:** Claude; **Harrington:** Thelma, Milford; **Hawley:** Sammy, Donald, William, Acel, Arlene, Joan; **Hiltz:** Harry, Ethel, Effie, Esther, Celia, Russell; **Hooper:** Juanita; **Houck:** Mildred; **Housten:** Anna; **Langley:** Ethel; **Lawrence:** Annabell, Fred, Charlie, Harry, Mable, Elizabeth; **Loomis:** Ellen, Clarissa, Darwin; **McNeil:** Ellen; **Miller:** Merral "Red", Edna, Nelda, Roy; **Miracle:** Bill; **Neville:** Nancy, Rockford; **Nichols:** George; **Parkinson:** EdWynna, Wayne, Janice; **Pettit:** Wayne, Alton, Elaine, Frone, Alvin, Eveline; **Polmanteer:** Almira; **Purks:** Bennie, Deforest, Heighter, Merlin; **Reilly:** Ella; **Rosebrugh:** Frank, John, Emma, Roxie; **Shattuck:** Blaine, Maxine; **Slater:** Vera; **Spearman:** Don; **Stotler:** Louella; **Sutton:** Cameron; **Turland:** Jim, Margaret; **Utter:** Clara; **Wiltse:** Earl, Clinton, Hazel, James, Minnie, Chester, Alvin; **Withey:** Anna Belle

In 1977, Bell school had a reunion and 32 families attended. They were the first country school to have reunions.

Margaret Turland's family bought and lived in the school after it closed.

Mae LaDue taught this school when it was a log cabin.

Jess Rittenburg and Frank Lovell were given the contract to build the school in 1907. It was to be 24 foot by 36 foot, with a stone walk. The building was to be brick veneer and double floored. It would have cedar shingles and contain 8 windows, three on each side and 2 in front.

There was a flag raising on November 9, 1934.

Cameron Sutton's family lived on a farm near the school. He had a standing of 90% when he graduated from the 8th grade in 1930.

BELL SCHOOL

BELL SCHOOL

County Schools

BELL SCHOOL

Teacher—Mrs. Kenyon.

We are preparing for Washington's birthday. The first and second grades are making booklets on George Washington. Mrs. Kenyon gave the third and fourth grades study booklets on George Washington. The fifth and other grades are preparing essays, each one writing, using a different topic, below is one of them, prepared by Minnie Wiltse, an eighth grade pupil:

Washington as a Leader and Soldier

George Washington became a leader and soldier in 1756 when he was in the French and Indian war which was before the Revolutionary war. Washington became the best general and commander in the whole thirteen colonies. He became a leader from Virginia in 1774 when he became delegate to Congress. When the time came to make an appointment for commander in chief of the Continental forces, Washington was appointed. He said he was greatly honored, but honestly felt that he lacked capacity for so great a task. Throughout he refused pay for the services.

Washington arrived in Boston early in July, 1775, after the battle of Bunker Hill. Beginning as leader with an army of fourteen thousand untrained men, with few supplies, he had not only to attend to his military duties, but to serve fourteen masters, Congress and the thirteen colonies, and to persuade all of them to support his operations and to furnish him with supplies. It was an experience to make a great man, to break a weak one. When in March, 1776, the British were driven out of Boston. Washington had become a statesman and a military commander of the first rank. But Washington's fame does rest on the battles he fought. The greatest battle of the Revolution—probably the decisive conflict that turned the tide of war—was the battle of Saratoga, at which Washington was not present. Nevertheless, Washington's retreat across New Jersey; the manner in which he turned and struck the pursuing enemy at Trenton and Princeton and then established himself on the heights of Morristown, overlooking New York; and the vigorous resistance to British occupation of Philadelphia, all marked him as a competent military leader. That record was crowned by the terrible winter at Valley Forge in 1777-78, when in spite of the misery of his soldiers, the clamor of the people tired of war, the delays of a fugitive Congress, and the intrigues to have him superceded he held his position and kept his starving army to its tasks.

When, on the news of the French alliance in 1778, Philadelphia was evacuated to unite the two British armies in New York, Washington chased the enemy across New Jersey and shut them in New York. There he remained watching and waiting on the Hudson river, while the British carried the war to the south. Three weeks later Cornwallis surrendered and the actual fighting was over. When officers of the army suggested that Washington use force to extort from Congress, their just dues and overturn their inefficient government, he sternly rebuked them. Like another Cincinnatus, he retired in 1783 to Mount Vernon—as he hoped, to private life. No one saw more clearly than did Washington, in the critical period from 1783 to 1789, the dangers which beset the New Nation, and it was largely owing to his efforts that a convention finally met in Philadelphia in May, 1787 to revise the articles of Confederation. In the convention Washington's influence was a prime importance. On the first day he was called to the chair by an unanimous vote, and during the four months session his hand guided the work of one of the most notable assemblies ever held. He later became the first president of the United States which was the thirteen colonies at that time.

BELL SCHOOL

We have four new pupils, Patricia, Leon, and Mervin Cornell, from Lupton school and Juanita Hooper from Midland.

We have started practicing for our Christmas program which will be given Dec. 23, at 8 o'clock. Everyone is welcome.

Seventh and eighth grade grammar class gave current events last Thursday.

Mrs. Dennis has been reading stories from books that she got at Teacher's Institute. First and second grades come to class with prepared lessons so that they can listen to the stories.

Our bulletin board is decorated with eskimos and snow houses.

We are glad to have two new shades at our windows.

A Thanksgiving dinner was given at school the day before Thanksgiving. Most of us decided that we had overeaten.

For the last few weeks we have been playing games for morning exercises.

Those being neither tardy nor absent since the beginning of the school year are: Elaine, Wayne, and Alton Pettit, Mable Lawrence, Merlin and Heighter Purks.

Teacher: Rosella Dennis

Reporter: Warren Davis

BELL SCHOOL

BELL SCHOOL

We have a trophy from the AA A club of Michigan for our work in safety this year.

The school board got us a new ball and bat which we appreciate very much. We are having lots of fun with them.

Little Nancy Neville of Niagara Falls, N. Y., visited our school Wednesday.

The fifth grade are making medieval village.

A photographer came to school Thursday. We enjoy having our pictures taken and hope they will be nice.

Mr. Rhodes came to explain about the summer 4-H projects. Three boys were interested in the forest-fire study.

The first grade made ducks and umbrellas for blackboard decorations. By standing on the table they could put them up themselves.

Mable Lawrence and Mina Fritz were absent Monday.

Miss Neal visited our school a little while.

Mrs. Migan is taking a group of children to West Branch for music rehearsal, Friday.

Editors —Upper grades
Teacher —Mrs. Migan

BELL SCHOOL

William and Sammy Hawley were absent Thursday.

The first grade is studying about a little boy whom lives in Mexico. His name is Pedro. They are making Mexican hats and coats.

The teacher finished reading "Moni the Goat Boy." It is by Johanna Spyri.

We have a new safety poster. It says: "Look at that skid It pays to be alert doesn't it Ace?"

The third grade is studying about birds. They are making booklets of different kinds of them.

We have a nice picture of lumbermens Memorial. It is in the Huron National Forest on the bank of the Au Sable river.

Mrs. Migan is reading "Uncle Tom's Cabin. It is a good story and we like it

Teacher —Mrs. Migan
Editors —Upper grades

BELL SCHOOL

The third grade has been studying out of the science stories for Language. They made some wind toys.

The teacher is reading Admiral Bobby by George Fraschel. Bobby is a little Liverpool street boy.

Some of the school is getting vaccinated. There are six of them. Their names are Bennie and Deforest Purks, Lillian, Mina and Stephen Fritz and Mrs. Migan, our teacher.

The fourth grade is learning some new poems and have them pretty good. Some names of them are "The Wonderful World", "The Whispers" and "Flags".

We are studying our songs. We all know them pretty well. Here is one of the songs.

The Dairy Maids

Evening light on the pasture land
Twinkling, twinkling,
Here we go with our pails in hand
Mary, Molly and I.

Cowbells ringing a sleepy chime,
Twinkling, twinkling,
While we call at the meadow thyme.
Mary, Molly and I.

Sweet and warm is the milk
We take every morning
When the children begin to wake,
Mary, Molly and I.

Making butter is the best of fun,
Churning, churning,
We're all sorry when summer's gone.
Mary, Molly and I.

Editors — Upper grades
Teacher — Mrs. Migan

THURSDAY, OCT. 27, 1938

BELL SCHOOL

Mr. Coulter visited us and we organized a 4-H Handicraft Club. William Hawley was elected chairman, Alton Pettit vice-chairmen and Donald Spearman, Secretary - Treasurer. We are collecting our materials and tools so we can work. We asked Mr. James Turland to be our leader.

Rev. Bryan of Selkirk and Rev. Daniel Whybren visited us this week. Rev. Whybren gave us a reading, "When the Minister Comes to Tea." We enjoyed it very much.

Alton Pettit brought a water lizard to school. It is about ten inches long. His father got it for him at the lake.

We have a flower garden in our school this year We have several kinds of flowers.

Mrs. Migan brought us two gold fish from Saginaw. They are interesting to watch.

Miss Neal called for a few minutes and told us that the local chapter of the Red Cross had presented us with a membership in the Junior Red Cross. She gave us the pins. We wish to thank the local chapter for our membership.

We have a portfolio of lovely Japanese pictures.

BELL SCHOOL

Back row:

Stephen Fritz, Don Spearman

Second row:

Merral "Red" Miller, Sammy Hawley, Bill Hawley, Wayne Pettit, Lillian Fritz, Annabell Lawrence

Third row:

Donald Hawley, unknown, Joan Fritz, Edna Miller, unknown

Front row:

Nelda Miller, Mina Fritz

BELL SCHOOL

Bell School

Churchill Township Hall was bursting with activity on July 25 when 105 former students of Sage Lake, Withey, O'Neil, Atherton and Red Schools gathered for the annual Bell School reunion.

Following a bountiful noon potluck, Mildred Houck Cross presided at the business meeting.

Gifts were presented to four former teachers who were present: Maude Embury, Jennie Cook, Grace Switzer and Lanora Markell. Also recognized were Ellen McNeil Warner for coming the farthest from Florida; Bill Miracle, 87, and Darwin Loomis, 84, eldest men; Ethel Langley, 86, eldest woman.

Officers elected for the coming year were: Mildred Cross, president; Bernadine Hiltz, vice-president; Dorothy Brindley, secretary; Geraldine Steward, corresponding secretary.

A grab bag exchange conducted by auctioneer Geraldine Steward wound up the day's activities.

The group plans to meet again the third Saturday in July, 1982.

Bell School Reunion 1977

The school bell rang again July 16 when the annual Bell school reunion was held at the Churchill Township Hall, Selkirk.

Former students, their families and friends (32 in all) started the festivities with a delicious potluck luncheon. A brief business meeting and program was conducted by retiring president, Mildred Houck Cross. Newcomers, William and Clara Utter, Jay and Linda Utter and Jessie Valley were welcomed. Clara Utter was elected president for the next three years. Leah Sullivan and Anna Blum entertained with a few readings. Mildred Cross gave the memorial reading in remembrance of Claude Hall, Russell Hilts and Florence Burns, who passed away since the last reunion.

Gifts were presented to Ethel Hilts Langely, 84, the eldest lady present; Chester Wiltse, 80, the eldest man; Mr. and Mrs. Darwin Loomis, longest married (58 years); Mr. and Mrs. Wayne Parkinson, who came the farthest from Bradenton, Florida; Mr. and Mrs. Cleon Pratt and Mr. and Mrs. Warren Davis, who got up the earliest to travel north for the occasion.

The program ended with a grab bag and the signing of cards for those ill and unable to attend.

Many old friends and teachers were sadly missed at this reunion, but there's always 1978, the third Saturday in July.

BELL SCHOOL

The school bell rings, and here we are. We have seven beginners. They are: Maxine Shattuck, Nelda Miller, Eveline Pettit, Donald Hawley, Janice Parkinson, and the twins, John and Joan Fritz. They have been learning to read cards and read from the board. They also have been making pictures and posting them on the bulletin board.

To start the new school year our school board bought us a new pencil sharpener, a new health ball, a tripod magnifier, library index cards, chalk, drawing paper and text books. We appreciate their generosity very much.

We have only one entrance to our building and as our windows are quite high from the ground, the school board decided we needed a fire escape for safety. So they got the material and Mr. Neville the janitor, built a fire escape that can be reached easily from the windows.

Mrs. Milgan brought a book, "The Knave of Hearts" to school and read it to us. It was beautifully illustrated by Maxfield Parrish. We enjoyed the play and the pictures very much.

The following was written by the fifth grade English class:

One day not long ago Blaine Shattuck brought us a box of sand. We wondered what was in it. He told us that there were live turtle eggs in the sand. He let us keep them at school. A few days after they began to hatch. We watched two baby turtles break out of the sand. In the night another one came out but we couldn't find it until we looked in the cold air register. There is was and didn't seem to be hurt. We keep them in a dish of sand that also has a dish of water. We copied a poem from the board and learned it. This is the poem:

My Turtle

My turtle is a tidy boy
For when he is tired of play,
He folds himself up carefully
And puts himself away.

BELL SCHOOL

BUSENBARK SCHOOL

Foster Township (Township 21 North Range 1 East)

NW1/4 of SW1/4 of Section 2 at Cabin Lake & Peach Lake Roads

Began operation 1909

Between 1909-1920, the school had three different locations in Horton Township, one of which was the corner of Peach Lake and Cabin Lake Roads.

BUSENBARK SCHOOL

Foster Township (Township 21 North Range 1 East)

NW1/4 of SW1/4 of Section 2 at Cabin Lake & Peach Lake Roads

Began operation 1909

Teachers:

1914 Margaret Rhinehart;   1934-1935 Gertrude Atherton;   1940-1941 Bernard Fegan

<u>Unknown dates:</u> Ethel Eckelson, Ida Olsen Perkins, Cora Newberry Richardson, Madaline Bennett, Marion Gray, Gertrude Carr Nieman, Mary Hartsell, Mary Richardson Myas, Viola Schick, Mr. Jardine

Students:

Ballard: Maude;   **Busenbark:** James, Florence, Margaret;   **Jardin:** Mernie, Lyman;   **Lewis:** Lera, Nita;   **Reinhart:** Margaret;   **Rich:** Kenny, Doris, Oney, Jennie

BUSENBARK SCHOOL

Information from a letter dated September 6, 1998 from Dean & Margaret Busenbark:

"The Busenbark School was originally located on the Wildview Farm, which was the home place of Lera Lewis (later Felsted and now Nelson) and her family. The building was later moved to one acre of property owned by Harry Busenbark, who was Superintendent of Schools. The property is located on Cabin Lake Road, east of Peach Lake Road.....later it was moved to its present site on Peach Lake Road, just south of Cabin Lake Road.....at least one of the moves was accomplished by rolling the building on logs from site to site."

Warranty Deed from Elihu W. Louthan, single man to School District #4, Twp. of Horton, Ogemaw County Dated 10/27/1915:

"One square acre of land in the northwest corner of the NW1/4 of SW1/4 of Section 2, T 21 N, R 2 E, Ogemaw County. This deed is executed to convey to said School District #4 for school purposes as long as same shall be used for school purposes by said School District, but in case of the removal of the school house to be built upon said land, and the discontinuance of said land for school purposes, that said land shall revert back to said grantor, his heirs and assigns."

BUSENBARK SCHOOL

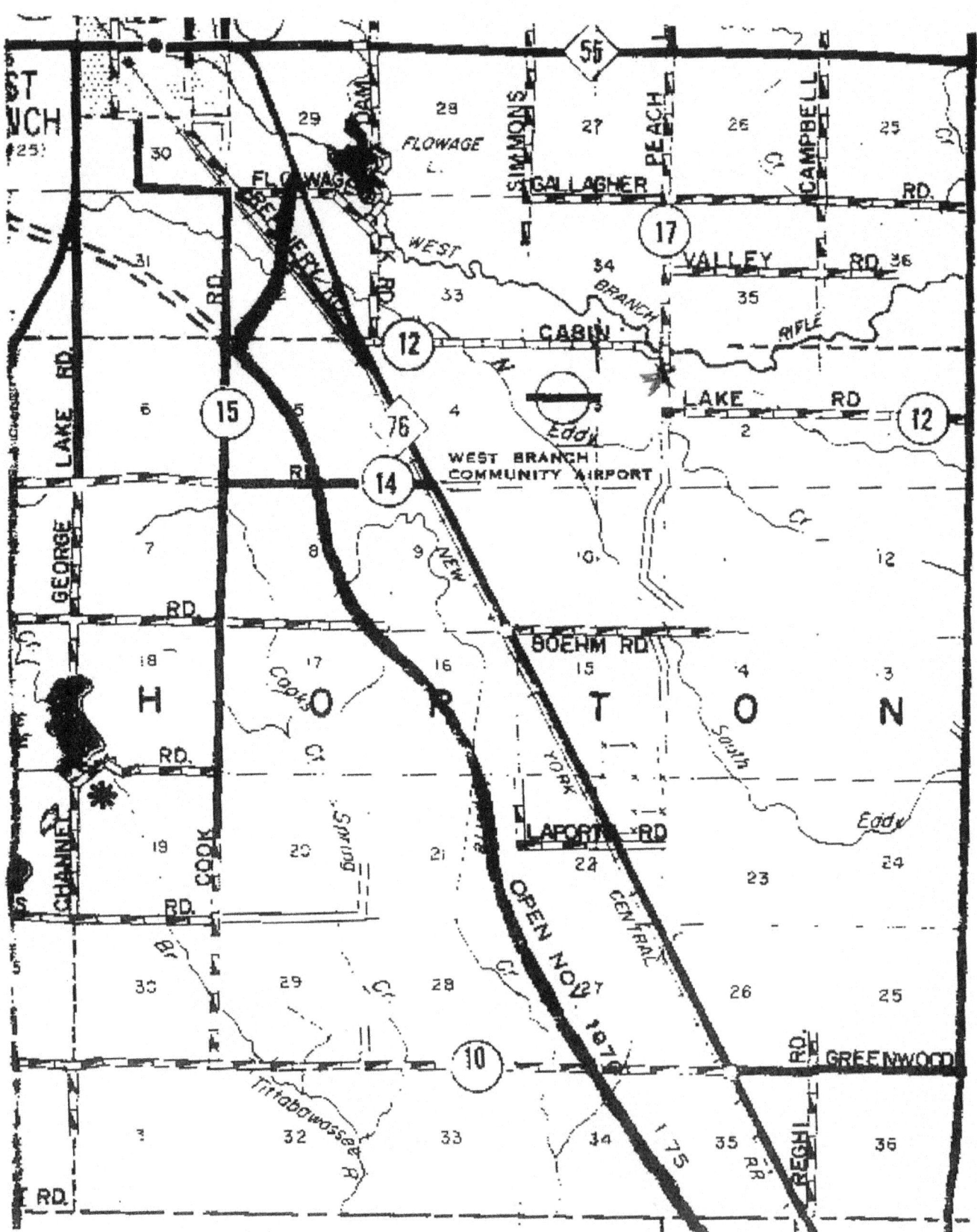

BUSENBARK SCHOOL
1914

Back row:

Maude Ballard, Oney Rich, Jenny Rich, Margaret Reinhardt (teacher), James Busenbark

Front row:

Doris Rich, Lera Lewis, Mernie Jardine, Nita Lewis, Florence Busenbark

Lyman Jardine, Oney Rich, Jenny Rich, Margaret Reinhardt, James Busenbark, Mernie Jardin, Doris Rich, Nita Lewis, Maude Ballard, Lera Lewis, Florence Busenbark

BUSENBARK SCHOOL

BUSH LAKE SCHOOL

Mills Township (Town 21 North Range 3 East)

NW ¼ of NW ¼ of Section 26 on Lucinda Drive

Ended 1936

Teachers:

1893 Margaret Mattel; 1923-1925 Edith Rusher; 1925-1926 Helen David; 1926-1927 Bernard Fegan; 1927-1928 Rose Walker; 1928 Hazel Brunges; 1934 Merle Matthews (replaced early); 1934-1935 Ethel Engel or Gertrude Atherton; 1936-1937 Cleo Priest; 1937-1938 Mrs. Meddler; 1938-1939 Berniece Pickens

Students:

Burch: Dorothea, Stella; **Cummings:** John, Robert; **Dobler:** Dorothy; **Goatbe:** Grace, Joyce, June; **Mallach:** Gwendolyn; **May:** Chester, Eunice; Moorehouse: Jack; **Parr:** Boyd; **Walter:** Clyde Junior; **Williams:** Donna, Marvin; **Zaidl:** Mike

BUSH LAKE SCHOOL

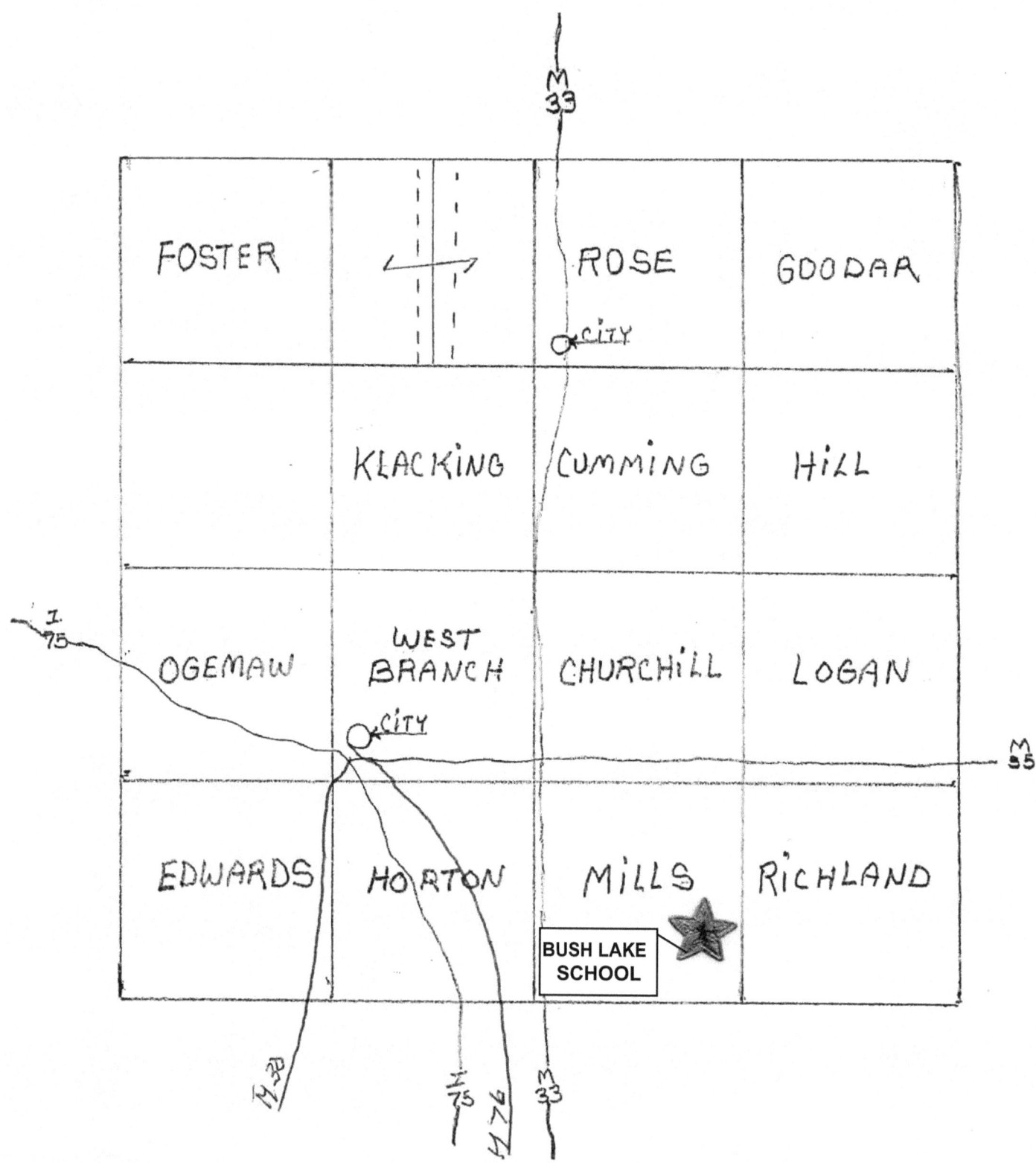

CAMPBELL CORNERS SCHOOL

West Branch Township (Town 22 North Range 2 East)

SE ¼ of NE ¼ of Section 11 at Campbell and State Roads.

Began operation in 1882

Consolidated with West Branch 1964

CAMPBELL CORNERS SCHOOL

Teachers:

1898 Lottie Jones; 1902 Fred Bullock; 1903-1904 Elizabeth Pillsbury Campbell; 1904-1905 Edward Scheele 1911 Margaret Mattel; 1916 Alice Lovell; 1927-1928 Vera Winter; 1928-1929 Hildreth Carscallen Webster; 1929-1930 Irene Miller McCoy; 1933-1941 Wenona Gibson; 1943-1944 Ivadelle Holshoe; 1944-1952 Maxine Barber Wangler; 1952-1953 Helen Evans; 1953-1955 Alice Selesky Thompson; 1955-1962 Maxine Wangler; 1962-1964 Dorothy Decker; <u>Unknown dates:</u> Ervadean Evans Wangler, Alla Norris, Loretta Reetz, Florence Freed Bennett, Pearl Rose Mason (1920's), Arzell Walker Williams, Wilma Oliver Crawford, William Fuhrman, Phoebe Regan McLeod, Florence Freed, Mac Humphrey (1946), Alma Hacht, Jenette Swift Ross (soon after 1884)

Students:

Adams: Alice, George, Vina; **Ammond:** Ora, Lizzie, Bert, Alice, Etta, Clyde, Roy; **Andrus:** Vera, Nelson; **Bagley:** Alice, Beth, Henry; **Baumchen:** Frank, Helena; **Beach:** Cora, Alex, Della; **Bedtelyon:** Don, Matt, Luke, Dean; **Bennett:** Harvey, Alberta, Johnnie, Minnie, Gladys, Frank, JoAnn, Gale, Hazel, Maggie, Alvin, Mary, Sam, Florence, Clara, Laura, Harold, Ruth; **Brick:** Mike, Dorothy, Marie, Gerald, Harold, Nancy, Nyla, Diane, Judy, Lizzie, Willie, Lucille, Clyde, Luella, Clarence; **Brindley:** George, Frank, Albert, William, David, Fred, Mable; **Campbell:** Harry; **Carscallen:** Hildreth, Irene; **Cascadden:** Mary, Marvin, Debbie; **Chase:** Charles; **Cody:** Edward; **Cool:** Eva, Charlie, Eldon; **Cross:** Ernest; **Denio:** Charles, Alice; **Denman:** David, Gaynol, Sonya; **Dennison:** Bertha, Arthur; **Dill:** Fred, Todd; **Dishaw:** Paul, Willie, Bertha, Joseph, Cliffie, Louis, Ben; **Ferguson:** Joyce, Joni; **Finerty:** Edward, Mamie, George, James, Patrick, John, Clarence; **Fisher:** Austin, Brayton; **FitzGerald:** Clyde, James, Rola, Burton; **Fornwall:** Emerson, Myrtle, Margaret, James; **Fournier:** Gary, Sandy, Randy; **Freed:** Oliver, Willie, Maria, Maudie, Florence, Jessie, Lizzie; **French:** Lizzie; **Gray:** Michael, Brian; **Green:** Alvena, Eugene, LaVerne; **Grossman:** Albert, Johnnie, Philip, Clyde; **Gruber:** Hazel; **Hacht:** Charlie, Maggie, Alma, Ada, James, Katherine, Frances, Florence, Fred, Edith, AnnaMae; **Harshman:** Hubert, Sharon, Doug, Todd; **Hart:** Mable, James, Malvin, Wilbur; **Headley:** Jessica, Mike; **Hendricks:** Henry, Della; **Herlick:** Arlene, Vivian; **Hodgson:** Frankie; **Holderied:** Joe, Mike, Philip; **Jameson:** Janet; **Krugh:** Emma; **Leonard:** Delbert; **Little:** Della, Emma, Jimmie, Helen; **Lovell:** Norman, Alice, Ruth, Kathleen, Russell; **Mackie:** Teddy, Richard, Hue; **Maxwell:** Randy, Leon;

CAMPBELLS CORNERS SCHOOL

Students (Continued):

McKinnon: Mary Ann, Jim, Margaret; **Mezzano:** Dennis; **Mier:** Ambrose, Frank, George, Arthur, Harold, Marie, Maggie, Gertie; **Morgan:** Harold; **Munn:** Diane, Sharon; **Muntz:** Myrtle; **Neubecker:** Raymond, Gladys, Robert, LaVern, Abbie, Lizzie, Emma, Leo, Pat, Helen, Joyce, Wanda, Jean, Bernice, Chuck, Ron, Willie, Jean; **Norton:** Patricia; **Nixon:** Harry; **Oyster:** Kenny, Carol, Verna; **Quick:** Ronald, Martha, Jerry, Janet; **Parliament:** Sydney, Nettie, Clara, Wesley, Devere, Kathy, Doug, Carol, Connie, Dwight, Delores, Leola; **Pepper:** Jeanette; **Philips:** Jennie, Peter; **Preston:** Ray, Bernice; **Reetz:** Edward, Margaret, Jack, Jane; **Rohl:** Fletcher, Mervyn; **Root:** Patricia; **Rosebrugh:** Allen, Lucie, Judson, Mark, Brenda, Reid, Carl, Earla; **St. John:** Pat, Karen; **Schalk:** Joey, Charmane, Mary, Shirley, Norman; **Schmitt:** Olith, Junior, Toby, Alice, Mary, Betty, Bob, Jerry, Dean, Aleen, John, Jake, Ethel, Marge; **Schneider:** Mary Ann; **Slater:** Charlie; **Smith:** John, Jane, Harold, Ethel; **Stanlake:** Frank, Oscar, Mae; **Stephens:** George, Evelyn, Joseph, Forest, Harold; **Striker:** James; **Thomas:** Geraldine; **Thorp:** Bob; **Trout:** Kathy, Debbie, Mike, Russell; **Turk:** Mary, Lena, Anna, Frances; **Valley:** Merritt, Mack, Mabel, Morris; **Voss:** Jan; **Wangler:** Nedra, Viola, Willard, Maxine, Marlene, Jane, Terry, Jeff, Gary, Jerry, Steve, Harold, Ronny, Dave; **Wilson:** Ella, Johnnie; **Wing:** Leslie; **Winters:** Alma; **Woodiwiss:** Johnnie, Nellie, Iva, Theodore; **Woughter:** Dennis, Larry, Jim, Daniel, Mark, Gerald; **Zettle:** Donald, Jerome, David, Greg

Jenette Swift taught in the 1880's. She also taught in a school called Whitman, but we have no information on a school by that name. She married James Ross, who taught at Ogemaw Springs in the 1880's.

Florence Freed is thought by her family to have taught in the first school in the wilderness north of Campbell School, where the Holy Family Cemetery is now located (1994). This may be the Whitman School for which we find no information.

In 1895, Campbell Corners was one of the largest country schools.

The school was destroyed by fire in November, 1947, and rebuilt with planned opening in the fall of 1948. In the meantime, classes were held in the old Stevens store, close to the old building.

For the school year, 1948-49, there were 45 students enrolled.

Ogemaw County Genealogical & Historical Society

CAMPBELL CORNERS SCHOOL

From the Ogemaw Republican, December 16, 1898:

<u>The School at the "Corners"</u> The school at Campbell Corners ranks among the largest in the county, and this year the attendance is somewhat increased. Miss Lottie Jones, of West Branch, is the present teacher in charge, and her efforts as an instructor are highly appreciated by the patrons of the school. The following is a complete list of the pupils attending:

George Stephens	Alma Hacht	Johnnie Woodiwiss
Harry Campbell	Nettie Parliament	Eddie Finerty
Mike Brick	Peter Philips	Frankie Hodgson
Ambrose Mier	Johnnie Grossman	Fred Dill
Charlie Hacht	Frank Brindley	Joe Holderied
Frank Mier	Clyde Fitz Gerald	George Mier
Albert Grossman	James FitzGerald	Ella Wilson
Norman Lovell	Judson Rosebrugh	Johnnie Wilson
Allen Rosebrugh	Harvey Bennett	Todd Dill
Abbie Neubecker	Morris Valley	Mamie Finerty
Maggie Hacht	Mack Valley	Bertha Dennison
Della Beach	Rola FitzGerald	Arthur Dennison
Maggie Mier	Burton FitzGerald	Paul Dishaw
Gertie Mier	Lizzie Neubecker	Willie Dishaw
Anna Hacht	Alberta Bennett	Bertha Dishaw
Cora Beach	Johnnie Bennett	Alex Beach
Alice Adams	Albert Brindley	Eva Cool
George Adams	Myrtle Muntz	George Finerty
George Brindley	Minnie Bennett	Frank Stanlake
Ada Hacht	Philip Grossman	Arthur Mier
Vina Adams	Henry Hendricks	Wesley Parliament
Maria Freed	Mabel Valley	William Brindley
Harry Nixon	Della Hendricks	Lizzie Freed
Maudie Freed	Alice Lovell	Nellie Woodiwiss
Lucie Rosebrugh	Clara Parliament	James Finerty
Jennie Philips	Emma Neubecker	

CAMPBELL CORNERS SCHOOL
About 1904

Teacher Alma Hacht

Front row, number 4 is Frank Baumchen, number 14 is Helena Baumchen.

CAMPBELL CORNERS SCHOOL
1904 - 1905

Pupils

- Fred Hacht
- Edith Hacht
- Maggie Hacht
- Anne Mae Hatch
- Lizzie Brick
- Willie Neubecker
- Lizzie Neubecker
- Willie Freed
- Oliver Freed
- Florence Freed
- Ray Perston
- James Striker
- Ora Ammond
- Lizzie Ammond
- Bert Ammond
- Alice Ammond
- Etta Ammond
- Oscar Stanlake
- Mae Stanlake
- Philip Grossman
- Clyde Grossman
- Eva Cool
- Charlie Cool
- Eldon Cool
- Teddy Mackie
- Richard Mackie
- Hue Mackie
- Mable Hart
- James Hart
- Malvin Hart
- Wilbur Hart
- Iva Woodiwiss
- John Bennett
- Minnie Bennett
- Hazel Bennett
- Maggie Bennett
- Alvin Bennett
- Hazel Gruber
- David Brindley
- Mable Brindley
- Albert Brindley
- Mary Turk
- Lena Turk
- Anna Turk
- Frances Turk
- Harold Smith
- Lena Baunchen
- Frank Baunchen
- Alice Bagley
- Beth Bagley
- Henry Bagley
- Alma Winters
- Alice Lovell
- Joseph Dishaw
- Cliffie Dishaw
- Mike Holdried
- Philip Holdried
- Jessie Freed
- Carl Rosebrugh
- Edward Finerty
- Patrick Finerty
- John Finerty
- Frank Stanlake
- Emma Krugh

1904 — 1905

Souvenir

CAMPBELL'S CORNERS PUBLIC SCHOOL

District No. 3,

West Branch Twp., Ogemaw Co., Mich.

ED. E. SCHEELE, Teacher

Peter Neubecker, — — Director
John Hacht, — — Moderator
Eb. Brindley, — — Treasurer

CAMPBELL CORNERS SCHOOL
About 1905

Teacher Alma Hacht

Girl with white collar is Helena Baumchen Bragg.

CAMPBELL CORNERS SCHOOL

CAMPBELL'S CORNERS PUBLIC SCHOOL

District No. 3

West Branch Twp., Ogemaw Co.,

Michigan

ALICE LOVELL, Teacher

School Officers

Sidney Carscallen	Director
Edward Brindley	Treas.
William Preston	Modr.

PUPILS

Mary Bennett	Ruth Bennett
Emerson Fornwall	Bernice Preston
Clyde Ammond	James Fornwall
Louis Dishaw	Ben Dishaw
Roy Ammond	Nelson Andrus
Sam Bennett	Hildreth Carscallen
Florence Bennett	Ruth Lovell
Willie Brick	Clyde Brick
Ernest Cross	Irene Carscallen
Myrtle Fornwall	Theodore Woodiwiss
Fred Brindley	Clarence Finerty
Vera Andrus	Delores Parliment
Clara Bennett	Kathleen Lovell
Lucille Brick	Luella Brick
Laura Bennett	Ethel Smith
Margaret Fornwall	Geraldine Thomas
Margaret Reetz	Clarence Brick
John Smith	Russel Lovell
Harold Bennett	Leola Parliament
Leslie Wing	

CAMPBELL CORNERS SCHOOL

CAMPBELL CORNERS SCHOOL
1929

Back row:

Dorothy Brick, Gladys Neubecker, Evelyn Stephens, Nedra Wangler, Marie Brick, Irene McCoy (teacher), Joseph Stephens, George Stephens, Edward Cody, Eugene Green, James Hacht, Donald Zettle

Center row:

Austin Fisher, Gerald Brick, Ray Neubecker, Harold Brick, Harold Mier, Olith Schmitt (Smith), Viola Wangler (Neubecker), Junior Schmitt, Della Little, Katherine Hacht, Gladys Bennett (Mason), Devere Parliament, Frances Hacht

Front row:

Florence Hacht, Charles Hacht, LaVerne Green, Willard Wangler, Jerome Zettle, unknown Jones, Marie Mier, Emma Little, Forest Stephens, Leo Neubecker, Brayton Fisher, Frank Bennett, Maxine Wangler

CAMPBELL CORNERS SCHOOL

CAMPBELLS CORNERS SCHOOL NOTES

Hello everyone.

We are back to school again after a weeks vacation for potato digging. Many of us are entertaining lame backs and are wondering if vacation pays.

We have the nicest new book, "Birds of America." It was given to us by the mothers in our district. We also are very proud of our scales. Thanks everybody.

Our reading nook is nearly completed. It's all red and black and very cozy. Come read with us some day.

The seventh and eighth grade have completed their circular charts of the early explorations in America.

We were very glad to have Miss Neal visit us one day last week. Come again.

The fourth graders have just returned from their journey to Belgian Congo. They're leaving next week for Arabia.

A new family moved in our school last week, Mr. and Mrs. Hornet and their thousand children. I'm afraid we're going to commit some crimes around here if they stay very long.

The fifth and sixth graders are busy improving their letter writing.

We have the most hectic school room this month. Cat's fighting, witches riding around on brooms, guns shooting, ducks falling, grinning yellow faces, and ghosts and goblins every where. Yes, October's the month.

We enjoyed a happy hour with Columbus today. We learned poems, read the story of his life and made some interesting posters about him.

Our posters for Oliver Wendell Holmes' poem the Height of Ridiculous are amusing and interesting. We enjoyed learning the poem.

Did you know that the normal pulse of a horse is from twenty eight to forty beats per minute?

CAMPBELL CORNERS SCHOOL

West Branch, Ogemaw County, Michigan   Thursday, July 22, 1948

New Building Ready Soon

—Photo by Awrey

Only ten days of work were required to complete all the cement block and floor work in the new Campbell's Corners School under construction to replace the old building destroyed by fire last November. All labor on the new edifice, that consists of one large study room, two cloak rooms, two lavatories, a hallway and a handicraft room, is being donated and is under the supervision of school-board members Don Reetz, Sam Munn and Mrs. Edward Wangler. The purchase of a piece of adjoining land known as the Joe Stevens property will enable the expected 30 to 35 students to enjoy a larger playground. Until the new building is completed, some time this fall, classes will continue to be held in the old Stevens store close to the other site.

CAMPBELL CORNERS SCHOOL

CAMPBELL CORNERS SCHOOL
1952 - 1953

CAMPBELL CORNERS SCHOOL
1954 - 1955

Top row:

Alice DeNio, Joseph Schalk, Martha Quick, Michael Brick, Alice Thompson (teacher), Norman Schalk, Sharon Harshman, Jerry Quick, Jane Reetz

Second row:

Edward Reetz, Sharon Munn, unknown, Wanda Neubecker, unknown, Kathy Parliament, (Unknown), Deanne Munn, Dean Bedtelyon

Third row:

Patricia Root, Daniel Norton, Carol Parliament, Helen Neubecker, Patrick Neubecker, Mary Schalk

Bottom row:

Ronald Quick, Mary Schmitt, Joyce Neubecker, Jeanette Pepper, Dennis Woughter, Patricia Norton unknown,, JoAnn Bennett, unknown Pepper, Daniel Woughter

CAMPBELL CORNERS SCHOOL
1958 - 1959

       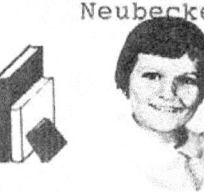 

Top row:

Jean Neubecker, Nyla Brick, Mark Rosebrugh, Chuck Neubecker, Dennis Mezzano, unknown, Janet Quick

Second row:

Jim Woughter, Wanda Neubecker, Brenda Rosebrugh, Maxine Wangler (teacher), Mike Brick, Bernice Neubecker, Gary Fournier

Third row:

Doug Harshman, Terry Wangler, Reid Rosebrugh, Bob Thorp, Pat St. John, Martha Quick

Bottom row:

Joyce Neubecker, Bob Schmitt, MaryAnn Schneider, Jerry Schmitt, Jerry Quick, Karen St. John, Daniel Woughter

The Country Schools of Ogemaw County: Volume 1

CAMPBELL CORNERS SCHOOL

Top row:

Martha Quick, Brenda Rosebrugh, Carol Parliament, Karen St. John, Wanda Neubecker, Bob Schmitt, Pat St. John, Jerry Quick

Second row:

Mike Brick, Doug Parliament, Bernice Neubecker, Reid Rosebrugh, Jim Woughter, Doug Harshman, Terry Wangler, Gary Fournier

Third row:

Connie Parliament, Jean Neubecker, Chuck Neubecker, John Smith, Mark Rosebrugh, Janet Quick, Nyla Brick

Fourth row:

Sandy Fournier, Ron Neubecker, Jim McKinnon, Helen Little, Kathy Trout, Jeff Wangler, Jane Smith

CAMPBELL CORNERS SCHOOL
1963-1964

Back row:

Jean Neubecker, Carl Rosebrugh, Randy Maxwell, Mark Rosebrugh, Jessica Headley, John Smith, Chuck Neubecker, Doug Parliament, Nyla Brick, Janet Quick, Dorothy Decker (teacher)

Second row:

Matt Bedtelyon, Mary Cascadden, David Zettle, Gary Wangler, Jan Voss, Jane Smith, Kathy Trout, Jeff Wangler, Gale Bennett, Ron Neubecker, Dave Wangler, Connie Parliament

Third row:

David Cascadden, Jerry Wangler, Steve Wangler, Debbie Cascadden, Joyce Ferguson, Mike Headley, Harold Wangler, Dwight Parliament, Debbie Trout, Randy Fournier, Mark Woughter, Kenny Oyster, Ronnie Wangler, Carol Oyster

Front row:

Greg Zettle, Joni Ferguson, Earla Rosebrugh, Luke Bedtelyon, Mike Trout, Diane Brick, Leon Maxwell, Judy Brick, Verna Oyster, Todd Harshman

CAVERLY SCHOOL

Logan Township (Town 22 North Range 4 East)

SW ¼ of NW ¼ of Section 9, State Road at Beach Road

Discontinued in 1935

Teachers:

1919-1921 Edith Crow;   1932-1935 Edith Crow (last teacher)

Students:

Bennett: Bill, Bob;   **Best:** Clifford;   **Caverly:** Warren, Calvin, Emery, Lawrence; **Diehl:** Betty;   **Schultz:** Howard;   **Taylor:** Charlotte;   **Wright:** William

CAVERLY SCHOOL

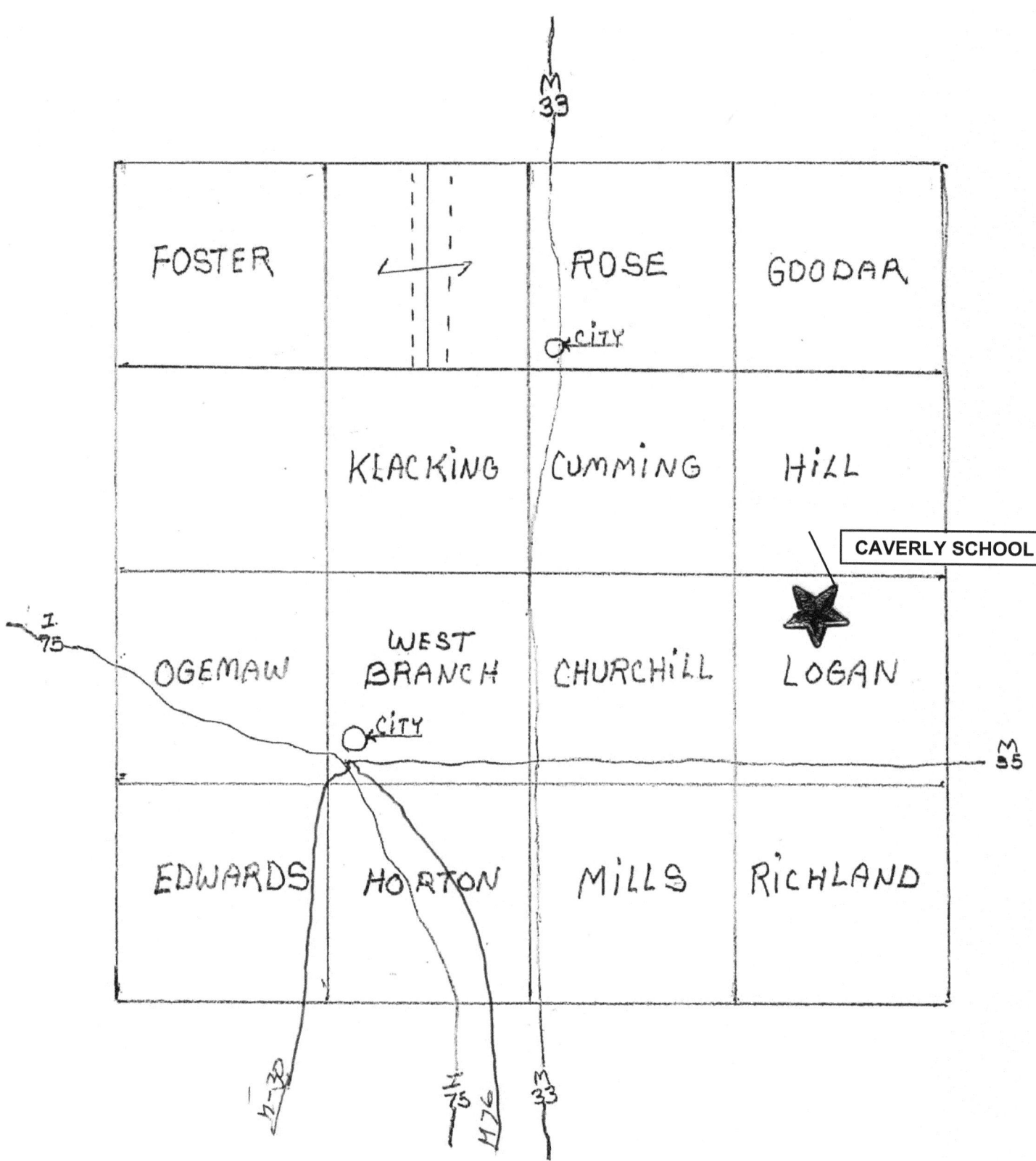

COOK SCHOOL

Horton Township (Town 21 North Range 2 East)

SW ¼ of NW ¼ of Section 8 on Cook Road

First year in use - 1889

Consolidated with West Branch Public Schools - 1964

COOK SCHOOL

Horton Township (Town 21 North Range 2 East)

SW ¼ of NW ¼ of Section 8 on Cook Road

Teachers:

1892-1898 J. E. Ford; 1912-1918 M. Babcock; 1918-1919 Cleo Woodiwiss; 1919-1921 Mina Goff; 1921-1923 Gladys Quackenbush; 1925 Francis M. Dennis; 1925-1926 Eva Nelson Madison; 1927-1931 Vera Winter Reetz; 1930-1934 Doris Rau; 1931 Margaret Husted; 1934-1937 Pauline Reiter; 1937-1944 Inez Lehman; 1944-1945 Florence Bishop; 1945-1948 Inez Lehman; 1948 Joan Green (sub for Inez Lehman Feb-May); 1948-1951 Loretta Morris; 1951-1954 Veronica Krengielski; 1954-1955 Muriel Hallgren Pekrul; 1955-1956 Anna Mae Reilly Illig; 1956-1961 Dorothy Decker; 1961-1962 Marie Buhlman; 1962-1965 Esther Bragg Rau <u>Unknown dates:</u> Helen Decker Church, Mary Dikos, Lucille Kennedy Hooper, Maxine Barber Wangler, Elizabeth Wilcox, Beatrice Belson

Students:

Barber: Bob; **Bender:** Lloyd; **Bennett:** John, Leo, Geraldine; **Bohnard:** Josephine, Rose, Joe; **Bray:** George, Jack; **Brindley:** Delores, Donna, Keith, Loretta, Larry, Junior, Raymond, Bob, Wanda, Margaret; **Brown:** Jinnie, Eddie; **Buhlman:** Gerald; **Bunting:** Roland, Raymond, Terry; **Cascadden**: Allen, Althea, Judy, Bill; **Chambers:** Lois, Lyle, Gloria; **Christ:** Sharon; **Clark:** Margaret, Patricia; **Combs:** Lorraine; **Cook:** Alvin, Arnold, Betty, Greg, Janice, Shirley, Leonard, Tammy, Robert, Stella, Willie, Anna, Fred, Ella, Mona, Billy, Ida; **Cool:** Doris; **Curtis:** Leith, Linda, Mike, Joe, Robert; **Diebold:** Maude, George, Pena; **Durfee:** Charlene, Harry, Sharon, Shelly, Neil; **Egan:** Caroline, Genevieve, Mildred; **Ehinger:** Betty, William Jr.; **Engman:** Emil; **Evans:** Gail, Janet, Karen, Kirk; **evens:** Eric; **Ewing:** Caroline, Clarence, Clayton; **Exelby:** Cindy; **Fell:** Carrie, Louise; **Finerty:** Katie; **Finnerty:** Etta, Abbie, Maude, Blanche; **Gehl:** Richard, Leo, Leon, John; **Gerber:** Eva; **Greer:** Karen, Larry, Tim; **Higgens:** Margarete, Vera; **Hoyer:** Dennis, Dick; **Illig:** Althea, Gary, Marsha, Larry, Linda; **Ingman:** Betty; **Jantzi:** Anna, Mary; **Kartis:** Francis; **Kauffman:** Adeline, Alvin, Barbara, Fannie, Floyd, Henry, Maud; **Kennedy:** Ferman, Charley; **King:** Mary, Rozella; **Knepler:** Anna, Francis, Mike; **Krug:** Willie; **Kuhn:** Cora, David, Debra, Hursel, Mary, Mona, Billy; **LaFountain:** Keith, Mary, Ellen ;**Lehman:** Dale, Jack, Jerry, Larry, Phyllis, Mike; **Lester:** Donald, Julie; **Link** Hattie, Fred, Martha, George; **Mackey:** Jay; **Martin:** Peggy, Anita, Stanley, Bill; **Melrose:** Doris, Howard, Phyllis, Tom; **Mier:** Larry, Kathy; **Miller:** Francis, Jim, Paul, William; **Morris:** Darrold Jr., Darrold Sr., Donald; **Most:** Mabel; **Muntz:** Frank, Alice, Ida; **Noel:** Bernard, Charlene, Dennis, Margaret, Mike, Paul; **Noffsinger:** Jerry, Jackie, Jim, Jo Ellen, Judy; **Oliver:** Alvin, Max; **Ouellette:** Mary; **Palm:** Philip; **Rau:** Bethal, Keith, Robert; **Raymond:** Betty, Bonnie, Jimmy; **Reed:** David, Donald, Mary, Ronald; **Regan:** Ned, Belle, Jennie, Ama;

COOK SCHOOL

Students (Continued):

Resteiner: John, Walter; **Safford:** Annella; **Scheele:** Bernard, Doris, MarjorieAnn, Helen Jane, Marlene, Ruth Ann, Flora, Priscilla, George, Eddie; **Scott:** Johnny, Larry, Sharon, Cloie, Addie; **Sharpe:** Minnie, Joe, Bert, Steve; **Sheil:** Jean; **Smaltz:** Frank; **Sperling:** Bernard, Linda, Terry; **Stamm:** Jim, Steven, Eddie; **Stevenson:** Lowell; **Strong:** Annie, Cherri; **Taft:** Erma, Terrance; **VanDyke:** Elly Jo; **Walters:** Judy, Louise; **Warren:** Betty, Robert, Ruth Ann, Sandra; **Werblo:** Joe; **Whitman:** Lena, Ross; **Wilkenson:** Conover, Jay, Marjorie, Zora; **Willett:** Dick, Linda, Nancy, Martha, Patricia, Rose Ann, Ronnie; **Winters:** Frank, Willie, Andrew; **Wirges:** Harvey, Jacob, Rose, Tillie, Mary; **Young:** Jeffery, Jessie, Jim, John; **Zettel** Bill, Rick; **Zettle:** Diane, Magdaline, Rozena, Regina, John; **Ziembo:** Charles, Julius

In 1898 the school officers were Jacob Zettle, John Regan, and Jacob Wirges.

Harvey Wirges was born on the Wirges farm on Cook Road in 1905. He received all of his schooling in the Cook school. He remembers that Helen Decker and Lucille Kennedy had been his teachers.

Bill Cascadden and Ray Brindley liked to wade in the creek behind the school. One day Bill tore his pants playing, and the teacher told him he could go home. He went to Ray, and tried to talk him into going with him, and instead of going home; they would go to the creek to play. Ray really didn't like to get in trouble, and he knew skipping school was not what he should be doing. But he really wanted to go with Bill. Then he decided that if his pants ripped, he too could go home. So, he ripped the seam of his pants and went to the teacher and told her he needed to go home, because he had ripped his pants. She let him go, and needless to say, the two boys spent the rest of the day playing in the creek.

Jack and Phyllis Lehman loved to tease their teacher, Mrs. Hallgren, about when she was going to get married. One day the teacher gave the two a ride home, and on the way they begin teasing again. She finally asked them if she invited them to her wedding, would they please quit teasing her about it. They agreed, and sure enough, the next summer, along came their invitation to the wedding.

COOK SCHOOL

Muriel Hallgren taught in Cook School, and remembers some of her best students. She named Allen Cascadden, Phyllis Lehman, Ruth Ann Warren, and Tammy Cook. The County Superintendent of Country Schools was Delia Neal Richardson, and her secretary was Dolly Martin. Hazel Cook was the president of the Cook School Board, with Nedra Lehman and John Scheele as the other two members.

The Cascadden children were expected to come straight home from school, and were given a time limit. They walked a half mile on Cook road, and then about a mile east on Rau. There was a great little creek, that was so much fun to play in, but if they came home wet, they were in trouble. At their house, like many other families, if they got in trouble in school, they were in worse trouble when they got home.

The schedule for the day at Cook School was: classes began at 9 a.m., at about 10:30 there was a 15 minute recess. At noon, the beginners were sent home for the day, and the rest of the students had an hour to eat and play. At 2:30 the first, second, and third grades were sent home, and the rest had a fifteen minute recess. At 4 p.m., school was out, and then it was time to clean the school. There were no janitors, students did the sweeping, black board washing, erasures cleaning, bathrooms tidied, etc.

On Valentine's Day there was a box to put the valentines in, and each student brought one for everyone. Jay Wilkenson used to bring heart shaped frosted cookies. They always looked so pretty before students got their hands on them.

COOK SCHOOL

The Christmas Program was a big deal each year. There was a small stage, with a sheet hung on wire to open and close. Most students had a piece to recite, and some also had parts in a play. It was such fun. Even the small children had something to do. At the end of the program, Santa always came with a box for each of us. It had peanuts and hard candy in it, and everyone was thrilled to get it.

For the school year 1927-28, the school Treasurer was Mr. Conrad S. Bender. The Bender family were a prosperous Amish family that lived on a farm near the school.

There were 32 students enrolled for the year 1948-49.

In 1991 there was a reunion of the Cook School students and teachers. This was organized by Leona Holt Cascadden, Howard Melrose and Althea Cascadden Phillips, the latter two being Cook School students for all their elementary years. Over 100 people attended. Eleven former teachers were there.

COOK SCHOOL
June 28, 1898

School District No. 2, ... Cook

... Township of Horton

* * * * *

School Officers:
Moderator....................JACOB ZETTEL
Director.......................JOHN REGAN
Assessor......................JACOB WIRGES

* * * * *

"Good Luck" will keep us over the ditch—if we jump hard. . . . . . .

* * * * *

TERM:—

Ending June 28th. 1898.

* * * * *

J. E. Ford, Teacher.

...PUPILS...

- Mary Wirges
- Minnie Sharpe
- Francis Kartis
- Josephine Bohnard
- Magdaline Zettel
- Ferman Kennedy
- Stella Cook
- Belle Regan
- Anna Knepler
- Cloie Scott
- Francis Knepler
- Hattie Link
- Katie Finerty
- Frank Winters
- Willie Winters
- Frank Smaltz
- Rose Bohnard
- Priscilla Scheele
- Fred Link
- Bert Sharpe
- Willie Cook
- Abbie Finnerty
- Ida Muntz
- Rose Wirges
- Steve Sharpe
- Joe Bohnard
- Andrew Winters
- Regina Zettel
- Eddie Scheele
- Addie Scott
- Fred Cook
- Maude Finnerty
- Ella Cook
- Tillie Wirges
- Ida Cook
- Robert Cook
- Jacob Wirges
- Ned Regan
- Frank Muntz
- Alice Muntz
- Rozena Zettel
- Charley Kennedy
- Maude Diebold
- Etta Finnerty
- Jennie Regan
- Flora Scheele
- Joe Sharpe
- Joe Werblo
- Margarete Higgens
- Lena Whitman
- Ross Whitman
- Vera Higgens
- Jinnie Brown
- Eddie Brown
- Anna Cook
- Martha Link
- George Diebold
- Willie Krug
- Carrie Fell
- Louise Fell
- George Scheele
- George Link
- Philip Palm
- Ama Regan
- Blanche Finnerty
- William Miller
- Pena Diebold
- Mike Knepler

COOK SCHOOL
1944 or 1945

Back row:

Helen Jane Scheele, Anita Martin, Betty Ingman, Zora Wilkenson, Doris Melrose, Tom Melrose, and Bob Barber

Center row:

Ruth Ann Scheele and Peggy Martin

Front row:

Howard Melrose, Phyllis Melrose, Donna Brindley, Rosie Willett, Keith Brindley, Loretta Brindley, and Bill Martin

COOK SCHOOL
1944

COOK SCHOOL
1951-1952

Top row:

Judy Cascadden, Lowell Stevenson, Caroline Ewing, Jack Lehman, unknown, C.J. Ewing, and Martha Willett

Second row:

Larry Scott, Jackie Noffsinger, Judy Noffsinger, and Raymond Bunting

Third row:

Phyllis Lehman, Jerry Lehman, Mike Noel, Charlene Noel, Paul Noel, Bill Cascadden, and Linda Willett

Bottom row:

Jerry Noffsinger, Jimmy Raymond, Jim Noffsinger, and Roland Bunting

COOK SCHOOL
Reunion 1991

COOK SCHOOL REUNION
HORTON TOWNSHIP HALL
SUNDAY AUGUST 11th
1:00pm – 6:00pm

Buffet Dinner

chicken
meatballs
ham
augration potatoes
potato salad
baked beans
pasta salad
fruit salad
jellow salads
relish tray
veg. dip
pickels / olives
rolls / bread & butter
coffee, tea, punch
cake

The response from our first mailing was outstanding, but now we need to know how many to plan dinner for. Please complete the attached form, cut on the dotted line and mail with your check or money order to Leona.
Note:
$5.00 per person is needed to cover the dinner and we will pass-a-hat to pay for the hall.

SEE YOU ON THE 11th.

Bring your snapshots or other memorabilia to share

COOK SCHOOL

Reunion 1991

Teachers at Cook School:

Mrs. Dorothy Decker
West Branch, Michigan

Mrs. Anna Mae Reilly Illig
Standish, Michigan

Mrs. Inez Allcock Lehman
North Port, Florida

Mrs. Helen (Decker) Church
West Branch, Michigan

Muriel Hallgren Pekrul
Indian River, Michigan

Mrs. Warren (Lucille Kennedy) Hooper
West Branch, Michigan
(Oldest at reunion - 98 years old)

Attending reunion:

Lucille Kennelly

Verna Winters Reetz

Inez Lehman

Loretta Morris

Mary Dikas

Muriel Halgren

Margaret Husted

Eva Nelson

Joan Green

Maxine Wangler

Vern Krienjietski

COOK SCHOOL
Reunion 1991

Margaret Brindley and eight of her nine children attended the 1991 Cook School reunion. In the back row standing, from left to right is: Loretta Brindley, Keith Brindley, Bob Brindley, Raymond Brindley, and Delores Brindley. Kneeling are Wanda Brindley and Junior Brindley. Seated is Margaret Brindley. This family won the prize for having the most members at the reunion. No one else came close. They also had the most students from one family in the school at any one time.

COOK SCHOOL
Reunion 1991

The gentlemen in the back row from left to right are: Howard Melrose, Bill Cascadden, Tom Melrose, and Allen Cascadden. The ladies in the front row are: Doris Melrose, Judy Cascadden, Althea Cascadden, and Phyllis Melrose. This was a large gathering in the Horton Township Hall, and a good time was had by all. People came from all over Michigan, and a few from out of state. Bill Cascadden got the prize for coming the farthest, from Texas. Many people have asked about having another, but no one volunteers to do the work.

COOK FAMILY
Ogemaw County Herald, 1994

Family picture

Gordon Cook of West Branch submitted this 76-year-old picture of a Cook family funeral in 1918. The family was gathered in honor of the late Robert Cook Sr. Pictured (left to right): Fred Cook and his wife, Hariet; Eva, Robert Cook's widow; Robert Jr.; George Cook's wife, Mattie; Ed Cook; George Cook; Al Slosser and his wife, the former Anna Cook; Ray Hatherly and his wife, the former Eva Cook; Otis Cook; Ted Cook; Bud Cook; and Eugene Cook (kneeling). Gordon Cook said his family came to this area from Canada around 1880.

Cook School and Cook Road were both named for this family. There were several members of the Cook family attending Cook School most of the time.

COOK SCHOOL

The Christmas program was always looked forward to with excitement. We were given Christmas poems to learn, and as we got older, we also had parts in the skits. A stage was built and sheets were hung for a curtain. The stage was very simple, and only came at the last minute. There was a Christmas tree, and the students made paper chains to hang. Names were drawn to give a small gift to. They were to be fifty cents or under. The teacher gave a small gift to each student. Santa Claus made an appearance at the end of the program. This is a picture of one Christmas program which feathered a group of first or second grade students performing "The Dance of the Paper Dolls". Six of the children were in the same grade. They were Judy Noffsinger, Carolyn Ewing, Judy Cascadden, Greg Cook, Eric Evens and Johnny Scott.

COOK SCHOOL

When Phyllis Melrose was ready to begin school, it was decided that there were too many students already for that class, so she stayed home for an extra year. When she started the following year, Keith Brindley also began. He only went a short time and it was decided that he needed to wait another year to begin. Phyllis then went through most of her time at Cook School with no other classmates.

She remembers each day beginning with the pledge to the flag, which at that time had forty-eight stars. This was, of course, before they added the words "under God." The teacher would begin the day reading from a book, perhaps a chapter a day.

Children in the beginner's class would go home at noon, and she had to walk home alone every day.

She remembers a big old furnace in the classroom, which was later moved to the basement. Not many of the schools had a full basement. Naturally the students were not to go down there without permission.

Games she played at school included; pom pom pull away, tag, anti I over, crack the whip, hide and seek, scrub (a softball game), the farmer in the dell, London Bridge, and ring around the rosie. Inside there was hide the thimble and I see something (name a color). There was a swing set for the younger children. Mrs. Morris introduced a new indoor game called clap in-clap out. This was for the older children.

A blessing was said before we ate lunch. We stood and recited, "thank you for the food we eat, thank you for the birds that sing, thank you God for everything." Others remember saying "for food and for thy gifts of love, we give you thanks and praise, look down, oh Father, from above, and bless us all our days."

COOK SCHOOL

When Phyllis was in the eighth grade, the county began to send the seventh and eighth grade students to the public school in West Branch. Until that time, students had gone through the eighth grade at Cook school, including her sister Doris, and her brothers Tom and Howard.

When Mrs. Loretta Morris was the teacher, she decided to try to raise the spelling scores for all the students. She divided the school into two teams, and each team recorded their Friday spelling score on a chart. At the end of the six week period, the scores were tallied, and the team with the highest score was the winner. The losing team had to host a pot luck supper for the winning team. It was fun for all, but I do not remember if the scores improved. I know that mine did not.

COOK SCHOOL

FOSTER		ROSE	GOODAR
	KLACKING	CUMMING	HILL
OGEMAW	WEST BRANCH	CHURCHILL	LOGAN
EDWARDS	HORTON	MILLS	RICHLAND

COOK

CRANBERRY LAKE SCHOOL
(Also known as HUGHEY LAKE SCHOOL)

Richland Township (Town 21 North Range 4 East)

SW 1/4 of NW 1/4 of Section 19

CRANBERRY LAKE SCHOOL

(Also known as HUGHEY LAKE SCHOOL)

Richland Township (Town 21 North Range 4 East)

SW ¼ of NW ¼ of Section 19

Teachers:

Pre 1913 Pearl Pillsbury; 1913-1915 Olive Pillsbury Sheldon; 1917 Ruth Shimmons Wilkinson; 1923-1924 Merle Martin; 1924 Howard Gregg; 1927-1928 Ethlyn Carpenter; 1927-1938 Bernard Fegan
<u>Unknown Dates:</u> Mrs. Black, Jennie Harrison (1914?)

Students:

Bentley: Margaret, John, Sarah; **Best:** George, Charles, Fannie, Hazel; **Dobler:** Arthur, Dorothy, Billy; **Earlie:** Nora; **Garish:** Rose; **Gibson:** Stella, George, Mary, Winona; **Kennedy:** Doris; **Kish:** Mary, Helen; **May:** Nellie, Loneta; **McDonald:** Harold, Alice; **Moorehouse:** Don; **Muzik:** Mike; **Pausits:** Frank, Raymond, Steve, Joe, Theresa; **Pinke:** Minnie, Margaret; **Runyan:** Fred, Rosie, Wilbur; **Simmons:** Margaret; **Van Meer:** Henry, Mary; **Walker:** Raymond; **Wickert:** Edna, Wilma, Stella; **Wilkinson:** Eugene; **Yates:** Walter

Students of Hughey Lake School 1933:

Alonzo: Margie; **Farro:** Bill, Irene; **May:** Betty, Loneta, Melvin; **Muzik:** Mary, John, Julia; **Pausits:** Steve, Joe, Theresa; **Simon:** Olga, Irma; **Steele:** Geraldine, Elmer; **Stephens:** Samuel; **Toth:** Elizabeth, Emil; **Valent:** John; **Vatter:** Clarence; **Zsidy:** Joe, Charles

Howard Gregg has accepted a position as a teacher of the Cranberry Lake School (once known as Hughey Lake School) as Merle Martin resigned to get married.

Fred Runyan attended Cranberry Lake School for seven years. After high school, he was persuaded to attend the Ogemaw County Normal, where he and Bernard Fegan were in a class with fourteen young women.

Rose Garish went to Cranberry Lake School when Bernard Fegan was the teacher.

When Cranberry Lake School was called Hughey Lake School, they had a Halloween party which was enjoyed by all.

In 1936 Hughey Lake School had eighteen students.

CRANBERRY LAKE SCHOOL
(Also known as HUGHEY LAKE SCHOOL)
1913-1914

Olive Pillsbury, Teacher

CRANBERRY LAKE SCHOOL
(Also known as HUGHEY LAKE SCHOOL)
1914

Bottom Row:

Unknown, Loneta (May) Valley, unknown, unknown, Harold McDonald, unknown, Henry (Hank) Van Meer

Second Row:

George Best, Stella (Gibson) Fegan, George (Hoot) Gibson, Ella unknown, Charles Best, unknown, Fred Runyan, unknown, Fannie (Best) Valent

Third Row:

Rosie Runyan, unknown, Mary Kish, Raymond Walker, Minnie Pinke, Walter Yates, Margaret Bentley, John Bentley

Fourth Row:

Hazel (Best) Vansickle, Don Moorhouse, Nora Earlie, Edna Wickert, unknown, Mary Gibson

Back Row:

Jennie Harrison (teacher), Margaret Pinke

CRANBERRY LAKE SCHOOL
(Also known as HUGHEY LAKE SCHOOL)
1917

Front Row:

Frank Pausits, Henry (Hank) Van Meer, Raymond Pausits, Fannie (Best) Valent, Alice McDonald, Helen Kish, Winona (Gibson) Netzloff, Nellie (May) Craner, Wilbur Runyan

Second Row:

Fred Runyan, Wilma Wickert, Stella (Gibson) Fegan, Loneta (May) Valley, George Best, Harold McDonald

Third Row:

Walter Yates, Stella Wickert, Rosie Runyan, Sarah Bentley, Mary Van Meer, Charles Best

Back Row:

Ruth (Shimmons) Wilkinson (Teacher), Minnie Pinke, Hazel (Best) Van Sickle, Edna Wickert, Margaret Bentley, Eugene Wilkinson, John Bentley

CRANBERRY LAKE SCHOOL
(Also known as HUGHEY LAKE SCHOOL)
1933

Front Row:

John Valent, Betty May, Margie Alonzo, Mary Muzik, Olga Simon

Second Row:

Bill Farro, John Muzik, Irene Farro, Bernard Fegan (teacher), Irma Simon, Elizabeth Toth, Julia Muzik

DALE SCHOOL

Rose Township (Town 24 North Range 3 East)

NE ¼ of NE ¼ of Section 32 on the corner of Heath and Reasner Roads

DALE SCHOOL

Rose Township (Town 24 North Range 3 East)

NE ¼ of NE ¼ of Section 32 on the corner of Heath and Reasner Roads

Teachers:

1886-1887 Rachel McKellar Howard; 1914 A. L. Dunlap; 1914 Mary Hammond; 1919-1920 Vera Parliament Hall; 1927-1928 Geneva Flynn Sarros; 1928-1929 Donna Nye; 1931-1933 Ada Fritz; 1933-1935 Coral Franklin; 1935 Harold Freeman; 1936-1938 Rosella Dennis 1939-1940 Lorene Blackledge <u>Unknown dates</u>: Emma Walker, Cora E. Jenson

Students:

Adkins: Ruth; **Alvord:** Richard; **Arntz:** Ruben, Johnny; **Arthur:** Frankie, Gerald; **Atherton:** Stella, Durfee, Johnie, Susie, Mary, Lillie, Rosie, William, Georgia, Olivia; **Bailey:** Georgie; **Bixby:** Bell, Herb; **Boddy:** Charles, Violet, Nina, Myrtle, Robert, Inez; **Boerner:** Ernie, Pearl; **Boreland:** Inez, Anna, Lottie; **Buck:** Clarence, Margaret; **Campbell:** Courtland, Hubert; **Carrington:** DeWitt; **Cheney:** Clarence; **Clark:** Bert; **Conley:** Clarence; **Cook:** Avis, Mary, Mayme; **Cornman:** Russell; **Corwin:** Marie; **Durfee:** Carl; **Duvekott:** Jenny, Mattie; **Eadey:** Gladys, Hazel; **Edmonds:** Edwin; **Emerson:** Beatrice, Imogene, Iris, Ila, Aleatha, Alma, Bulah, Thomas, Waldo, Juliaetta; **Fayette:** Gracie, Lydia, Mary; **Franks:** Vernon; **Graber:** Leo; **Hawley:** Agnes, John, Clinton, Elaine, Norman; **Ingram:** Ida, Orvin, Truman, Clara, Laura, Sarah, Hamilton; **Kinsey:** Alma, Lena, Viola; **Laberge:** Fred, Rocky; **Lalonde:** Joseph, Levi, Viola, Edith, George; **Leathorn** Velma; **Lewis:** Fannie, Mary; **Lockwood:** Roy, George, Edith; **Mailloux:** Virgie, Rosa; **Marion:** Laurence, Beulah, Berneatta; **Matthews:** Stanley; **Mayhew:** Reva, Twila, Wayne, Betty, Del, Andy; **McCracken:** Glen, Lucy; **McDonald:** Clyde, Jessie; **McKellar:** Rachel, Donald, Mable, Agnes, Alvin, Helen; **Miller:** Jay, Mirl; **Moore:** Martha, Hazel, Ida, Jennie, Mary; **Myers:** Lula; **O'Farrell:** Earl, Elmer; **Oyster:** Anna, Irvin, Mabelle, Beulah, Ralph, Earl; **Pawson:** Phebe, Ray; **Pollington:** Anna; **Porter:** Charley, Jake, Willis, Wm.; **Rank:** Martha; **Rankin:** Crystal; **Reasner:** Raymond; **Reed:** Lucille; **Smith:** Cora, Gertie; **Spafford:** Mina, Minnie; **Stinson:** Bertie, Jimmie; **Suggum:** Ada; **Talbot:** Johnie, Ida, Abbie, Ada, Dora; **Tanner:** Jay; **Teeple:** Gladys, Lawrence; **Thayer:** Geo., Jane, Myrtle, William; **Turley:** Mary, Elsie, Grace, Leeds; **Waite:** Alice; **Ware:** Jesse, Lloyd, Elsie, Ray; **Wilder:** Leslie; **Zimmerman:** Eudoras

Ada Fritz caught the mumps from one of her students, and was very sick.

DALE SCHOOL
1896-1897

Names of Pupils.

Jennie Moore	Ida Moore
Mary Moore	William Atherton
Rosa Atherton	Lily Atherton
Stella Atherton	Rosa Mailloux
Virgie Mailoux	Mina Spafford
Minnie Spafford	Jessie McDonald
Clyde McDonald	Laura Ingram
Hamilton Ingram	Sarah Ingram
Clara Ingram	Trueman Ingram
Anna Boreland	Lottie Boreland
Abbie Talbot	Dora Talbot
Ada Talbot	Ida Talbot
Alice Waite	Georgie Bailey
Fannie Lewis	Mary Lewis
Clinton Hawley	Agnes Hawley
John Hawley	Bulah Emerson
Alma Emerson	Thomas Emerson
Mary Fayette	Lydia Fayette
Gracie Fayette	Wm. Porter
Willis Porter	Charley Porter
Jake Porter	Rocky Laberge
Fred Laberge	Jimmie Stinson
Bertie Stinson	Myrtle Thayer
Jane Thayer	William Thayer
Geo. Thayer	Cora Smith
Gertie Smith	Eudoras Zimmerman
Phebe Pawson	Ray Pawson
Gerald Arthur	Bert Clark

Souvenir
Dale School.
— District No. 1 —
Rose Township,
Ogemaw,
Mich.
1896-'97

Presented by
A. L. DUNLAP, Teacher.
Board of Education: Wm. Talbot, Jas. Ingram, J. H. Spafford

DALE SCHOOL

Top Row:

Gracie Fayette, Stella Atherton, Truman Ingram, Ida Talbot, Clara Ingram, Mrs. Emma Walker (teacher), George Bailey, unknown Durfee, Lillie Atherton, Rosa Atherton

Bottom Row:

Johnie Atherton, Roy Lockwood, unknown Elvoid, Olivia Atherton, Johnie Talbot, Orvin Ingram, Ada Suggum, Bell Bixby, Frankie Arthur, Herb Bixby, unknown Elvoid, Susie Atherton (Buck)

DALE SCHOOL
Unknown Date

DALE SCHOOL
Unknown Date

Dale School

District No. 1.

Rose Township, Ogemaw County, Michigan.

Cora E. Janson, Teacher.

H. Oyster, Director.   C. Atherton, Moderator.

I. Oyster, Treasurer.

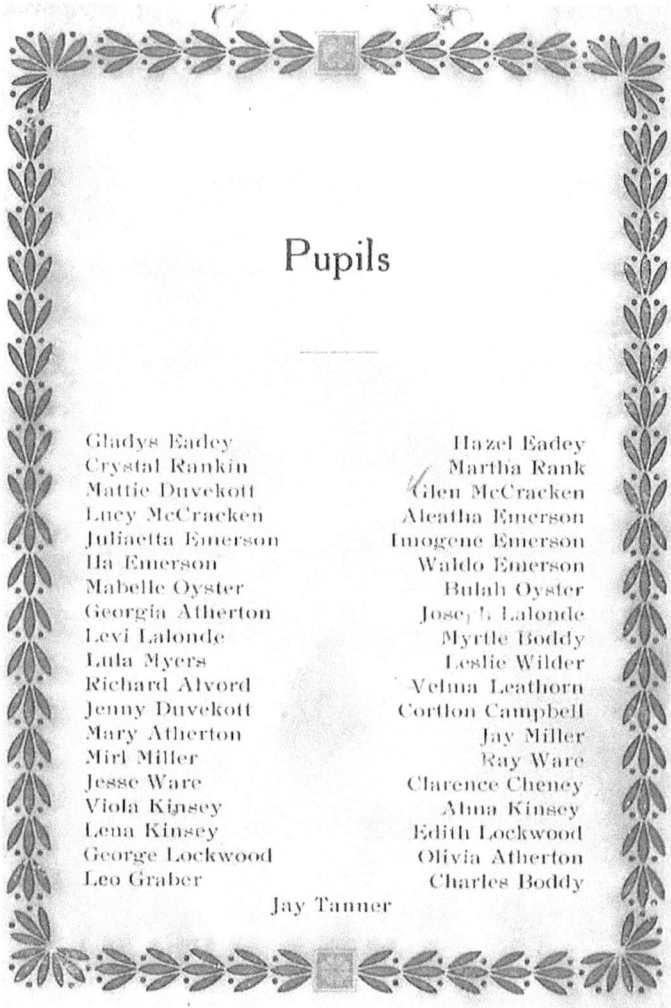

Pupils

Gladys Eadey
Crystal Rankin
Mattie Duvekott
Lucy McCracken
Juliaetta Emerson
Ila Emerson
Mabelle Oyster
Georgia Atherton
Levi Lalonde
Lula Myers
Richard Alvord
Jenny Duvekott
Mary Atherton
Mirl Miller
Jesse Ware
Viola Kinsey
Lena Kinsey
George Lockwood
Leo Graber

Hazel Eadey
Martha Rank
Glen McCracken
Aleatha Emerson
Imogene Emerson
Waldo Emerson
Bulah Oyster
Joseph Lalonde
Myrtle Boddy
Leslie Wilder
Velma Leathorn
Cortlon Campbell
Jay Miller
Ray Ware
Clarence Cheney
Alma Kinsey
Edith Lockwood
Olivia Atherton
Charles Boddy

Jay Tanner

DALE SCHOOL
Unknown Date

DALE SCHOOL
1914

Back Row to Front:

Charles Boddy, Clarence Conley, Mrs. Boddy, Violet Boddy, Mrs. Reasner, Unknown, Nina Boddy, Mrs. McKellar, Unknown, Anna Oyster, Andy Mayhew, Leeds Turley and baby, Stanley Matthews, Mr. Dougal McKellar, Myrtle Boddy, Mary Hammond (teacher), Mrs. Arntz, Mrs. Turley, Mary Turley, Unknown, Mrs. Ware, Rachel McKellar, Unknown, Irvin Oyster, Mrs. Billy Mayhew, Robert Boddy, Ruben Arntz, Jesse Ware, Dewitt Carrington, Raymond Reasner, Donald McKellar, Ray Ware, Vernon Franks, Courtland Campbell, Elsie Turley, Lola Boreland, Beulah Marion, Mabelle Oyster, Anna Pollington, Beatrice Emerson, Beulah Oyster, Grace Turley, Mable McKellar, Imogene Emerson, Unknown, Unknown, Johnny Arntz, Agnes McKellar, Laurence Marion, Carl Durfee, Alvin McKellar, Ralph Oyster (bow tie), Earl Oyster, Lloyd Ware (hat on), Ernie Boerner (white hat), Berneatta Marion, Inez Boreland, Inez Boddy, Pearl Boerner, Iris Emerson, Elsie Ware, Helen McKellar

DALE SCHOOL
1931 - 1933

Ada Fritz (teacher); some students include Reva Mayhew, Lawrence Teeple, Twila Mayhew, Wayne Mayhew, Gladys Teeple, Betty Mayhew, Clarence Buck, Avis Cook, Mary Cook, Mayme Cook, Russell Cornman, Ruth Adkins, Martha Moore, Hazel Moore

DALE SCHOOL

In disrepair, the school was torn down in 2004

The Country Schools of Ogemaw County: Volume 1

DAMON SCHOOL

Foster Township (Township 24 North Range 2 East)

SW ¼ of SW ¼ of Section 8 on Fairview Road

DAMON SCHOOL

Foster Township (Township 24 North Range 2 East)

SW ¼ of SW ¼ of Section 8 on Fairview Road

Teachers:

1881 Mrs. Bennett; 1882 Mary Miller; 1884-88 Harriet Snyder; 1885 Bertha Gates; 1886 Mattie Blakley; 1888 Linis Addison; 1889 George McCallum; 1889 Fred W. Dankin; 1892 Pearl E. Kennedy; 1893 Lizzie Paddison <u>Unknown date:</u> Flora Scheele, Neva Dobson Rakestraw

Students:

Bell: Clyde, Daisy, Ella, Charles **Cook**: Myra, Czar **Diamond**: Lottie **Drummond**: Florence **Hagerman**: Oscar **Harbell**: William **Lomason**: Ella, Grover, Joseph, Julia **McGregor**: Martha, Merrian, Merritt, Robbie **Quackenbush**: Althea **Sage**: Lizzie **Van Marten**: Adelbert **Woodrow**: Eddie, Maud, May

The Damon school was built in the spring of 1881. The school board director at that time was Orin Cook. A total of $75.76 was spent on the materials to build the school. The list does not include furniture, but does mention a pail and 4 dippers. The first term began on the first Monday of September, and Mrs. Bennett was hired for the three months for a total of $36. Three of the students were Althea Quackenbush, Lottie Diamond, and Myra Cook. This was three of the families who came from the southern part of the state to homestead in what was to become Foster Township. All three of the girls were in the first graduating class of the West Branch High School.

Damon teacher contracts: Bertha Gates in 1885 was paid $70 for 3 and ½ months. Harriet Snyder in 1886 was paid $28 per month. Mattie Blakley in 1887 was paid $288 for 9 months. George McCallum in 1888 was paid $87 for 3 months. Fred Dankin in 1889 was paid $130 for 3 months.

DAMON SCHOOL

George McCallum was a member of the first graduating class of West Branch High School and went on to become a teacher at the Damon School.

By 1916, Josephine Woods was County Commissioner, and in charge of the country schools for at least ten years.

A school year was three terms, beginning in September through November, then December through February, and finishing up with March through May. Teachers were not hired for a year but for each individual term. Sometimes there were three different teachers in a school year. The average age of the teachers was sixteen. As more schools were built, they changed to hiring for a whole year.

To teach in the country schools in 1881, you only needed to pass an oral examination proving your competency in reading, writing, and arithmetic. Althea Quackenbush remembers taking the exam, and it was a few arithmetic problems, read a few paragraphs, and then prove you could write well enough. Young women who finished high school, and had not found a marriage partner, often taught a few years first. Many would board with the families of their students.

A teacher's contract set out the duties of teaching, keeping accurate records, keeping the school clean, keeping the fire going in the winter, the pail full of drinking water, and many other duties that teachers do not have to do today. There were rules about proper behavior for teachers, and they were often asked to participate in church duties, as the services were usually held in the school buildings. One large expectation of the teachers was to get the students passed the 8th grade exam needed to get into high school.

DAMON SCHOOL

THE OGEMAW COUNTY HERALD

Mrs. Holt Tells of Early Schools in Foster Township

"Foster had the honor of being the first district school to send pupils to the local high school and I was one of them," remarked Mrs. Holt, the honored guest of the class of 1890 and was one of the three pupils from Foster Township to enter the West Branch High School.

When asked about her life in that area, she told a very interesting story.

"You know I grew up with Foster Township, saw its school built and saw its decline."

Mrs. Holt was born in Wayne County in 1874. Her father, a farmer, read of the wonderful opportunities in Ogemaw County. At that time circulars were distributed stating that 160 acres of land would be given to any family, who would build a home and reside there for five years.

"This sounded like a fortune to my father, so he and half a dozen neighbors came north to stake their claims. My father came about two months before the family came. He started to build the log house which he made from trees in the area."

In March, 1879, she, with her mother and brother, arrived at Beaver Lake Station, which was 13 miles from her new home.

"When I got off the train, I landed right in the middle of a snow bank. From the station, I rode on a sleigh to a logging camp near our home. I stayed here until our house was completed."

Within two years, 20 families settled in the area and a school was built. At the age of seven she began life in a rural school.

About this time the people thought they would like some recognition, so they presented a signed petition to the county board asking to become a township. This was accepted. The residents chose the name of Foster in honor of the newly elected governor of Ohio.

At the April election, someone was hired to clean the school, a date was also set for the first day of school, which was usually the following Monday. The school term ended in November.

"We were very fortunate, we always had good teachers. Anyone who could pass an oral examination, was eligible to teach. The requirements were to do a few problems, read a few paragraphs and write fairly well. Very little was taught besides reading, writing and arithmetic. The average age of our teachers was about 16 years.

My parents, like the rest of the neighbors, endured many hardships. Epidemics, the poor land and early frosts forced the families to leave one by one. About the time I entered high school my parents also left their 160 acres.

"My family moved into West Branch, where I graduated from the tenth grade and began my teaching career."

Today Foster township transports their pupils into the West Branch school and the place which was once her home is government owned.

DECKERVILLE SCHOOL

Rose Township (Town 24 North Range 3 East)

SE ¼ of SE ¼ of Section 15 on Deckerville Road

Transported to Lupton in the 1940's

DECKERVILLE SCHOOL

Rose Township (Town 24 North Range 3 East)

SE ¼ of SE ¼ of Section 15 on Deckerville Road

Teachers:

1911 Ethel Thompson; 1918-19 Velma Crawford Bemis; 1927-28 Bessie Whiteside; 1929-31 Inez Noffsinger Lehman; 1934-35 Louise Lince; 1935-36 Myrtle Lince; 1936-37 Edward Papp; 1937-38 Gertrude Atherton; 1939-41 Mary Edwards Fuhrman <u>Unknown dates:</u> Ruth Chambers, Beryl Reid, Lena Raymoure

Students:

Anderson: Jack, Marilyn **Byce:** Arlene, Vivian **Clare**: Mary **Fox:** Sydney, Virginia, Lela, Vera, Henry, Manley, Sharrow **Kalmbach:** Margaret **Mannore:** Ollie **Matthews:** Don, June, George, Reva, Oliver, Lawrence, Bill **Newcombe:** Billy, Carl **Oyster:** Lloyd, Virgil **White:** Marion, Russell

EASTSIDE SCHOOL

West Branch Township (Town 22 North Range 2 East) SW

First year of operation 1901

Relocated 1903

Consolidated with West Branch Public Schools 1964

EASTSIDE SCHOOL

West Branch Township (Town 22 North Range 2 East)

SW ¼ of SW ¼ of Section 25 at Campbell and Gallagher Roads

Teachers:

1888 Thomas Ballantine; 1888 Mrs. J. W. Morrison; 1888 E. M. Harris; 1889 Effie G. Wood; 1890 E. M. Harris; 1890 Mamie Merrill; 1891 Myrta Gillam; 1892 Marion Green; 1892 Ada Buckingham; 1893-94 Margaret Husted; 1894-96 Fanny Warren; 1895-96 F. A. Merrill; 1896-97 Vynne Buckingham; 1898-99 Suzie Richardson; 1899 Emma Husted; 1902 Margaret Husted; 1902-03 Gertrude Carr; 1904 Margaret Montell Kennedy; 1913-14 Cora Newberry Richardson; 1915 Mrs. Smith; 1916-1917 Edward Scheele; 1918-19 Mary Richardson Myas; 1922-23 Norma Nelson; 1923-24 Blanche Rau Thomas; 1924-28 Miss Eva Nelson; 1928-29 Edwina Parkinson; 1929-30 Jennie Norris; 1930-35 Francis Nelson Butler; 1935-36 Ada Fritz; 1936-39 Irene Nelson; 1939-40 Betty Candy Robinson; 1940-41 Irene Nelson; 1942-46 Donna Valley Nelson; 1946-51 Edwin Shiel; 1952-58 Marion Snyder; 1960-61 Virginia Simmons Clark; 1961-67 Rosella Dennis
<u>Unknown dates:</u> Helen Decker, Miss Brown (40's), Florence Andrews, Orville Cummings, Linda Black

Students:

Allen: Judy, Jim, Janet **Andrews:** Nancy, Sally **Barber:** Delma, Ellsworth **Beals:** Rosemary **Beck:** Richard, Don **Benjamin:** Ronald, Carol, Beverly, Gary **Bennett:** Betty **Bentley:** Vivian, Vinton, Vera **Black:** Sue, Nancy, Don, Linda **Bohlinger:** Verl, Melvin, Keith **Bradley:** Harold, Kenneth **Brewer:** Diane **Brindley:** Charles, Harold **Broberg:** Elaine **Buckingham:** Clyde, Janice, John, Ellis, Floyd, Bonnie, Bobby, Lyle **Carr:** Lynn **Clayton:** Jerry, Davis **Cook:** Harold **Cooley:** Hazen **Cross:** Maurice **Crow:** Edith, Junior, Evan **Cummings:** Shirley, Carol, Maxine **Dahl:** William **Daymon:** Ivan, Earl Jr. **Detzler:** Bill, Sue **Doron:** Isadore, Patience, Beatrice, Olive, Louis, Mary, Elinor **Down:** Mary **Drumm:** Chuck **Dunlap:** Harold, Juanita, Levere, Lucille, Quincy **Elmore:** Emma, John **Fahrner:** Lloyd **Ferguson:** Joyce, Brent

(Continued on next page)

EASTSIDE SCHOOL

Fisher: Robert, Eulalia, Betty, Nora, Jack **Folsom**: Charles **Fry**: Arthur **Gallagher**: Angeline, Thomas, Ruth, Joe, Wilson, Lawrence, Art, Marjorie, Marie, Pat, Gary, Danny, James, Linda **Gambler**: Laverne **Gray**: Louann **Grenier**: Diane **Grezeszak**: Albert **Griffin**: Erma **Grow**: Marion **Hamilton**: Bud, Sheri **Hart**: Leona, Opal, Juanita, John, Grace **Hennen**: Hilda, Vera, Maurice, Lois, Marjorie, Dorothy, Joan, Bernice, Gladys, Maureen, Mark, Cecil **Husted**: Ester, Helen, Gladys, Russell, Ailene, Margaret, Betty, Chuck **Klemmer**: Kurt **Kroll**: Nellie **Lang** Julia, Edmund, Rosa, Albert, Junior, Mary, Walt, Clara; **Livingood**: Bernice, Beatrice **Lucas**: Jeff **McAllister**: Nanette **McIntyre**: Verlyn **McLean**: Don, Gary; **Meir**: Philip Jr., Gerald, Lloyd, Irene **Mier**: Dorothy **Miller**: Sandy **Mogg**: Mary Jane **Morris**: Daisy, Eugene, Burt, Joyce, Tom **Nelson**: Louis, Irene, Alice, Robert, Carol Jean, Karen, Richard, James, Alma **Neubecker**: Joan, David, Ron, Larry, Ruth Ann **Newberry**: Harold **Ostrander**: Frank, Augusta, Delores, Donald, Edwin, Dallas, Eva **Oyster**: Carol **Parliament**: Brenda, Dwight **Parrish**: Betty, Ronald, Raymond **Peck**: Bonnie **Perkins**: Helen, Ray, Ralph, Dorothy, Annabelle, Kenneth, Betty, Delbert **Perry**: Carol, Betty Gean, Earl Jr., Mary Lou, Shirley Ann **Poling**: Frank, Paul, Mary Ida, Tom, Stacy **Priest**: Lee **Reinhardt**: Eugene, Emma, Alice, Edwina **Richardson**: Jack, Ben, Keith, Theodore **Robinson**: Sheila **Scott**: Lorraine **Sedore**: Hallie, Nora, Dorothy, Ralph **Selmes**: Donna **Seltz**: Vicky **Shepherd**: Amber **Siegle**: Mary, Edna, Elizabeth, Everitt **Simpson**: Billy **Sleeman**: Erma, Betty, Richard, Barbara **Slosser**: Joyce **Smith**: Mike **Stech**: Ernest Jr., Lowell, Rosemary **Steelman**: Gloria, Bill, Kay, Don **Stringer**: Jimmy, Barb **Sutherlund**: Art Mildred, Roy, Floyd, Albert, Ernest, Carl, Mary, Harold, Inez **Tabaca**: Eugene **Tabor**: Gene **Taylor**: Floyd, George **Thompson**: Lois **Trout**: Debbie, Diane **Valley**: Vivian, Donna, Norine, Abner **Vandenberg**: Harold, Howard, Donna **Walker**: Wayne, Delbert **Wangler**: Bernard, Jackelyn, Dallas, Helen, Ronnie, Mary Lou **Wilcox**: Lyle **Williams**: Garnet, LeRoy, Ray **Wilson**: Kathleen **Winter**: Ned, Clyde, Henrietta, Merceda, Jack, Marion **Zahm:** Raymond, George

EASTSIDE SCHOOL

This school was first located at Peach and Gallagher Roads and called District #5. A new school was built in 1904 and located at Campbell and Gallagher Roads.

Ed Scheele taught the 7th and 8th grade students to drive.

The school was closed for a week in February, 1924, due to the bad roads and the illness and death of the teacher's sister.

Erma Sleeman graduated from Eastside School on June 6, 1930 with a 96% average. Her teacher was Jennie Norris.

One evening this week (October, 1923) Miss Nelson, teacher of the Eastside School entertained students from four grades in her home.

On the Friday before Christmas in 1923, Miss Norma Nelson had her Christmas program, which was very well attended.

EASTSIDE SCHOOL
1912 or 1913

EASTSIDE SCHOOL
1913-1914

Miss Newberry, teacher

Class List:

Russell Husted, Thomas Gallagher, James Gallagher, Mary Dorpn, Helen Perkins, Emma Reinhardt, Elinor Doron, Mary Siegle, Everitt Siegle, Abner Valley, Isadore Doron, George Taylor, Harold Brindley, Ray Perkins, Floyd Taylor, Bernice Livingood, Edwina Reinhardt, Alice Reinhardt, Julia Lang, Edmund Lang, Laverne Gambler, Vivan Valley, Edna Siegle, Mildred Sutherland, Mary Lang, Janice Buckingham, Ray Williams, LeRoy Williams, Vera Hennen, Hilda Hennen, Gladys Husted, Beatrice Doron

There were two Sutherlands, a Livingston and a Bradley whose first names were not remembered.

EASTSIDE SCHOOL
Possibly 1913 or 1914

EASTSIDE SCHOOL
1915

Top Row:

Mildred Sutherland, Angeline Gallagher, Julia Lang, Mrs. Smith, Mary Down, Mary Siegle, Ester Husted, Emma Reinhardt, Helen Perkins, Isadore Doron, Harold Bradley, Laverne Gambler, Thomas Gallagher, Edmund Lang, Hazen Cooley, Floyd Taylor, Ned Winter

Center Row:

Patience Doron, Janice Buckingham, John Buckingham, Mildred unknown, Edna Siegle, Beatrice Doron, Elizabeth Siegle, Alice Reinhardt, Edwina Reinhardt, Rosa Lang, unknown, Helen Husted, Gladys Husted, Hilda Hennen, Leona Hart

Bottom Row:

Russell Husted, Ray Perkins, Clyde Winter, Garnet Williams, LeRoy Williams, Vivian Valley, Harold Cook, Henrietta Winter, Ruth Gallagher, Vera Hennen, Clyde Buckingham, unknown, unknown, unknown Sutherland, Kenneth Bradley, Ralph Perkins, Albert Lang, Ray Williams

EASTSIDE SCHOOL
1916 - 1917

Teacher: Ed. Scheele

EASTSIDE SCHOOL
1920's

Elaine Broberg circled girl in second row from front

EASTSIDE SCHOOL
1924

Back Row:

Walt Lang, Louis Nelson, Joe Gallagher, John Buckingham, Frank Ostrander, Roy Sutherland

Second Row:

Ellis Buckingham, unknown, unknown, Lyle Wilcox, Robert Fisher, unknown Gamber, Erma Sleeman, Ruth Gallagher, unknown, Olive Doron, Hallie Sedore, Nellie Kroll, Floyd Sutherland, unknown, Norma Nelson (teacher), unknown

Third Row:

Verl Bohlinger, Albert Sutherland, Maurice Hennen, Maurice Cross, Wilson Gallagher, Daisy Morris, Nora Sedore, Augusta Ostrander, Irene Nelson, Merceda Winter, Edith Crow, unknown, Dorothy Sedore

Fourth Row:

Ernest Sutherland, Lawrence Gallagher, Floyd Buckingham, Art Gallagher, Lois Hennen, Marjorie Hennen, Jack Winter, Jack Richardson, Ben Richardson, Carl Sutherland, Ralph Sedore, Alice Nelson, Mary Sutherland, Lynne Carr, Eulalia Fisher, Betty Fisher, Dorothy Hennen

EASTSIDE SCHOOL
1927

Back Row:

Jack Winter, Jack Richardson, Floyd Buckingham, Maurice Cross, Ellis Buckingham, Ernest Sutherland, Ben Richardson, Carl Sutherland, Robert Nelson

Second Row:

Clara Lang, unknown, Erma Sleeman, Eva Nelson (teacher), Augusta Ostrander, Daisy Morris, Edith Crow, Mary Sutherland, Alice Nelson

Third Row:

Jack Fisher, Junior Lang, Cecil Hennen, Keith Richardson, unknown, Lyle Buckingham, Donald Ostrander, Harold Sutherland, Wayne Walker

Front Row:

Gladys Hennen, Donna Valley, Betty Fisher, unknown, Lynne Carr, Marjorie Hennen, Delores Ostrander, Inez Sutherland, unknown

EASTSIDE SCHOOL
1931

Back Row:

Opal Hart, Marjorie Gallagher, Delores Ostrander, Marie Gallagher, Lynne Carr, Marjorie Hennen, Juanita Hart, Frances Nelson Butler (teacher), Carl Sutherland, Lawrence Gallagher, Jack Richardson, Melvin Bohlinger, Robert Nelson, Jack Winter

Middle Row:

Harold Vandenberg, Donna Valley, Dorothy Perkins, Joan Hennen, Junior Crow, Keith Richardson, Harold Sutherland, unknown, Howard Vandenberg, Donald Ostrander, Lee Priest, Harold Newberry

Front Row:

Bernice Hennen, Donna Vandenberg, Ailene Husted, Gladys Hennen, Eugene Morris, Annabelle Perkins, Wayne Walker, Theodore Richardson, Betty Sleeman, Eugene Reinhardt, Nora Fisher, Keith Bohlinger, Delbert Walker, Norine Valley

Ogemaw County Genealogical & Historical Society

EASTSIDE SCHOOL
September, 1935

STUDENT	GRADE	AGE	STUDENT	GRADE	AGE
Bohlinger, Keith	8	13	Crow, Junior (Evan)	6	11
Dahl, William	4	12	Gallagher, Marjorie	8	13
Hart, Grace	6	11	Hart, Opal	7	14
Hennen, Bernice	5	9	Hennen, Cecil	7	14
Hennen, Gladys	7	12	Hennen, Joan	3	8
Mier, Dorothy	8	14	Morris, Burt	B	6
Morris, R. Eugene	6	10	Nelson, A. James	6	10
Ostrander, Donald	8	14	Perkins, Annabelle	6	11
Perkins, Dorothy	6	10	Perkins, Kenneth	3	8
Perry, Carol Edward	B	5	Perry, Betty Gean	5	10
Perry, Mary Lou	3	8	Perry, Shirley Ann	2	7
Poling, Mary Ida	B	6	Richardson, Theodore	5	9
Reinhardt, Eugene	5	9	Sleeman, Betty J.	8	12
Sleeman, Barbara	4	9	Sleeman, Richard	3	8
Valley, Abner	3	8	Valley, Norine	5	9
Wangler, Bernard	3	8	Wangler, Mary Lou	2	6
Perry, Earl Jr.	3	8	Barber, Delma M.	7	14
Barber, Ellsworth D.	1	7	Stech, Ernest Jr.	5	11
Stech, Lowell	3	10	Stech, Rosemary	3	8
Daymon, Ivan	2	9	Daymon, Earl Jr.	B	5
Dunlap, Harold E.	2	8	Dunlap, Juanita	7	13
Dunlap, Levere	5	12	Dunlap, Lucille	8	14
Dunlap, Quincy M.	2	7	Beals, Rosemary	8	13
Meir, Philip Jr.	1	7	Meir, Gerald F.	B	5

EASTSIDE SCHOOL
1936

EASTSIDE SCHOOL
1936
Music Festival

EASTSIDE SCHOOL

Back Row:

Irene Nelson, Bernard Wangler, Abner Valley, Burt Morris, Kenneth Perkins, Erma Griffin, Joan Hennen, Joyce Morris, Joan Neubecker, Mary Lou Wangler

Front Row:

Betty Husted, Stacy Poling, Billy Simpson, Raymond Zahm, Mary Ida Poling, Betty Parrish, Bellistine, Jackelyn Wangler, Betty Perkins, Paul Poling, Tom Poling, Margaret Husted, Helen Wangler

EASTSIDE SCHOOL
May, 1946

Back Row:

Betty Perkins, Helen Wangler, Shirley Cummings, Lorraine Scott, Carol Cummings, Ronald Parrish, Dallas Wangler, unknown, Donna Valley Nelson (teacher)

Second Row:

Unknown, Margaret Husted, Edwin Ostrander, unknown

Third Row:

Verlyn McIntyre, Dallas Ostrander, Ronald Benjamin, unknown, Raymond Parrish, Delbert Perkins, Carol Jean Nelson, Louis Doron

Front Row:

Unknown, Jimmy Stringer, Charles Folsom, Gloria Steelman, Karen Nelson

EASTSIDE SCHOOL
1948

Back Row:

Shirley Cummings, Vivian Bentley, Lorraine Scott

Second Row:

Louis Doron, Edwin Ostrander, Carol Cummings, Ronald Parrish, Nancy Andrews, Margaret Husted

Third Row:

Dallas Wangler, Vinton Bentley, Emma Elmore, Raymond Parrish, Sally Andrews, Vera Bentley, Dallas Ostrander

Fourth Row:

Charles Folsom, Ronald Benjamin, Gloria Steelman, Mary Jane Mogg, John Elmore, Delbert Perkins

EASTSIDE SCHOOL
1952 - 1953

Top Row:

Mrs. Snyder (teacher), David Neubecker, Sue Black, unknown, Judy Allen, Chuck Husted, Maureen Hennen, Bill Steelman, Mary Jane Mogg

Second Row:

Pat Gallagher, Kathleen Wilson, Bud Hamilton, Eugene Tabaca, Marion Grow, Gary Gallagher

Third Row:

Lois Hennen, Ron Neubecker, Carol Benjamin, Bonnie Buckingham, Don Mclean, Beverly Benjamin

Fourth Row:

Gary Benjamin, Nancy Black, Larry Neubecker, Bonnie Peck, Bobby Buckingham, Barb Stringer, John Hart, Kay Steelman, Richard Beck

Bottom Row:

Don Black, Don Beck, Gene Tabor, Louann Gray

EASTSIDE SCHOOL
1954 -1955

Top Row:

Mrs. Snyder (teacher), Gary Gallagher, Linda Black, Danny Gallagher, Beverly Benjamin, Don Steelman, Lois Hennen, Richard Nelson, Maureen Hennen

Second Row:

Lloyd Fahrner, Ruth Ann Neubecker, Bud Hamilton, Don Mclean, Barb Stringer, Don Beck

Third Row:

Nancy Black, Bobby Buckingham, Bonnie Buckingham, Marion Grow, Jerry Clayton, Carol Benjamin

Fourth Row:

Pat Gallagher, Diane Trout, Jim Allen, Marion Winter, Bill Steelman, Sheri Hamilton, Davis Clayton, Kathleen Wilson, Richard Beck

Bottom Row:

David Neubecker, Larry Neubecker, Gene Tabor, unknown Mclean, unknown, Gary Benjamin, John Hart

EASTSIDE SCHOOL
About 1956

Don Steelman, David Neubecker, Pat Gallagher, Bill Steelman, Lloyd Fahrner, Bonnie Buckingham, Sue Black, Mrs. Snyder (teacher), John Hart

EASTSIDE SCHOOL
1961

Pat Gallagher, Marion Grow, David Neubecker, Maxine Cummings, Bill Steelman, Bonnie Buckingham, John Hart

EASTSIDE SCHOOL
1961

Beverly Benjamin, David Neubecker, Maureen Hennen, Gary Gallagher, Don McLean, Bill Detzler

EASTSIDE SCHOOL
1963

Lois Hennen, Sheila Robinson, Sue Detzler, Lloyd Meir, Irene Meir, Gary Benjamin, Barb Stringer

EASTSIDE SCHOOL

1966 - 1967

EDWARDS SCHOOL

Edwards Township (Town 21 North Range 1 East)

SW 1/4 of SE 1/4 of Section 26 on Greenwood Road

Built in 1902, consolidated with West Branch Public Schools 1964

EDWARDS SCHOOL

Teachers:

Early 1900's Margaret Beemer Hewitt; 1903-04 Olith Tesch; 1905-06 Edward Scheele; 1906-08 John Angerer; 1912-13 Vera Shrigley; 1913-14 Amy Richardson Husted; 1918-1919 Muriel Flint; 1919 Margaret Beemer; 1922-23 Florence Holt; 1924 Edward Foster; 1925-30 Florence Andrews; 1931 Kathleen Williams Witherspoon; 1932-33 Georgina Richardson; 1934-36 Leota Williams; 1935-41 Robert DeMatio; 1943-44 Edwin Shiel; 1947-49 Ruth Kleehammer; 1949-51 Florence Bishop; 1953-55 Helen Artman; 1955-57 Ruth Kleehammer; 1957-59 Anna Mae Illig; 1962-63 Marie Buhlman; 1960-62 Betty Candy Robinson; 1962-63 Evelyn Schneider Rau Unknown dates: Ada Johnson Link, Mary Loop Loney, Mr. Redmond, Alice Williams, Maggie McCauley, Jessie Shepherd

Students:

Alpin: Devere, Gilmore, Vivian, Don, Bernice **Anderson:** Lucile, Clara, Grace, Robert, Michael, James, Bessie, Jack, Helen **Andrews:** Harriett, Florence, Leo, Orrissi, Bessie, Stanley **Barcia:** LeRoy, Tom, Marg **Barley:** Alpha **Barringer:** Charlotte, Lucile, Clifford, Kenneth **Beckwith:** May **Beemer:** Marguerite **Bennett:** LeRoy, Gerry, Kenneth, Judy, Butch, Geraldine, Leo, John **Bernor:** Alfred, Ruth **Beyerlein:** Arnold, Kathy, Diane, Bill, Judy, Sandy **Blakely:** Elna **Bohnard:** Genevieve, Rosena, Beulah, Monroe, Lucille, Frank **Bowditch:** Marilyn, Donald, Danny **Bowsher:** Earl **Brownley:** Clyde, Mildred, Cyril, Lester **Buckel:** Russell, Ed, Bob **Burt:** Gladys, John, Bill, Margaret, Irwin, Helen, William **Buyea:** Grace **Carpenter:** Grace, Mame **Chapman:** Bob, Elsie, Peggy, Ruby, David, Phyllis, Marjorie **Chatterson:** Bill **Clayton:** Grace, Billy, Peter, Sadie, Carl, Gordon, Helen, Doris, Paul, James, Russel, Arzel, Elton, Margaret **Cohoon:** Claud **Cooper:** Lawson, Edgar, Eva, Bennie, Floyd **Cruickshank:** Roy, Billy, Leland, Lula, Jim, Edna, Gordon, Fred, Clair, Keith **Darling:** Iva, Elizabeth **Decker:** Angie, Mamie, Lucille, Gertrude, Ethel, Eathel, Walter, Flossie, Clair, Oscar, Goldie, Bruce, Glen, Elmer, Irene **DeClute:** Ida **Doer:** Chuck **Dunn:** Don, Judy, Bonnie, Dick, Cecil, Leonard, Doris, Karl, Carla, Kent, Kurt **Ehinger:** August, Darrel, Ronald, Debbie, Tony **Ellis:** A. Jay **Evilsizer:** Don, Phyllis, Dale, April **Ferguson:** Ralph **Flint:** Muriel **Flory:** June **Fournier:** Theodore, Eileen, Greg, Clarence, Teresa, Lillie, Idabel, Georgina, Gerald, Napoleon, Junior **Fuller:** Mamie **Galbraith:** Helen, Wesley **Gannon:** Roy

EDWARDS SCHOOL

Students (continued):

Gerber: Pete, Elizabeth, Daniel, Amos, Solomon, David, Moses **Gibson:** Esma **Gildner:** Herbie, Cecil, Roy, Doug, Marjorie, Catherine, Jeanette, David, Mary, Alex, Lucy, Valentine, Lucinda, Clarence, Hilda **Green:** Gertrude, Chloe, Irene, Joe, Byron **Griffith:** Sadie **Hacht:** Greg **Hamilton:** Gordon, Orville, Lucille, Mable, Lorn, Hazel, Rhonda, Lynn, Orthella, Ruby, Nauman, Irene, Gladys **Hepner:** Leo, Gladys, Gale **Hill:** Pearl **Hollowell:** Elsie **Illig:** Annamae, Marsha, Linda, Larry, Gary, Althea **Kaiser:** Floyd **Kelsey:** Dan, Geraldine, Delores, Floyd, Leon **King:** Orie, Bob, Donald, Bernice, Jack **Klug:** Fred, Terry, Steve **Lantern:** Mike **Little:** Ernie, Tim, Herb, Mike **Loop** Fred **Mackey:** J.D., Linda, Sue, Jay **Madden:** Beatrice, Florence **Martin:** Greg **McCauley:** Sam, Howard, Carl, Tom, Keith, Connie, Maggie, Jennie **miles:** Glen, Florence **Mutch:** Otis **Nagy:** Mary Jane **Nichols:** Grace **Noel:** William, Charles, Tom, Bobby **Oliver:** Adam, Max, Ernadine, Joan, Joyce, Alvin **Osborne:** Junior **Palinski:** Barbara **Pfeiffer:** Leonard, Harold, Norman, Harvey **Poplawski:** Richard **Poyner:** Edward, Linda **Prevo:** Joe, Shirley, Lester **Przylubski:** Barbara **Rau:** Gerald, Julie, Jeri **Reese:** Carl **Rhines:** John, Butch, Mona, Charles **Rose:** Joseph **Ruegsegger:** Doris, Katherine **Rundel:** Ona, Joseph, Wesley **St. John:** Flora, Grace **Schliter:** Connie, Bob **Sergent:** Kathryn, Ben, Joyce, Phyllis, Jim, Jack, Gary, Jean, Jay, Walter **Sias:** Mirinda **Spahn:** Leo, Audrey, Donna **Stone:** Clara, Edward, Lee, John **Stringer:** Maggie **Sutton:** Ronald, Crandall, Donna **Tank:** Clayton, Beverly **Timlick:** Lila, Betty **Tolfree:** Marie **Tupper:** Robert, Belle, Blanche **Tuttle:** Dorothy, DeWayne **Utter:** Sharon, Almeda, Sandra, Oka **Wade:** Helen, Margaret, Howard, Duane, Clair, Warren **Wallar:** Dewey, Hazen **Walls:** John, Max **Walters:** Stanley **Williams:** Thelma, Alma, Clarabelle, Bernadene, Warren, Charlotte, Lucy, Cora, Faye, Donald, Catherine, Leota, Boyd

1903-04 School Officers were Director Charles R. Hamilton, Moderator A. H. Flint, and Treasurer Sam McCauley.

The Edwards School was one of the very few schools in Ogemaw County where at one time the 9th grade was taught.

Four families had three generations in the school. They were the Sam McCauley's, the Warren Wades, the Frank Bohnard's, and the Tony Ehingers.

There were four one room schoolhouses in Edwards Township; Rau, Erb, Stillwagon and Edwards.

EDWARDS SCHOOL

1903 - 1904

SCHOOL DISTRICT
NUMBER ONE
EDWARDS, Ogemaw Co., MICHIGAN

September 14, 1903 — June 14, 1904

Presented By
Miss Olith N. Tesch
Teacher

SCHOOL OFFICERS

Chas. R. Hamilton	Director
A. H. Flint	Moderator
Sam McCauley	Treasurer

Pupils

Bessie Anderson	Grace Anderson
Lucile Anderson	Mamie Fuller
Clara Stone	Clyde Brownley
Charlotte Williams	Warren Williams
Esme Gibson	Elna Blakely
Otis Mutch	Oscar Decker
Clare Decker	Marguerite Beemer
Samie McCauley	Maggie McCauley
Jennie McCauley	Eva Cooper
Lawson Cooper	Edgar Cooper
Sadie Clayton	Peter Clayton
Nauman Hamilton	Clarence Fournier
Lillie Fournier	Bennie Cooper
Flossie Decker	Walter Decker
Floyd Cooper	Idabel Fournier
Ruth Bernor	Goldie Decker
Glen Decker	Flora St. Johns
Grace St. Johns	Jay Ellis
Johnie Gildner	Herbie Gildner
Valentine Gildner	Alfred Bernor
Orrissi Andrews	Leo Andrews
Bruce Decker	Ida DeClute
Pearl Hill	

P. A. OWEN PUB. CO., DANSVILLE, N. Y.

The Country Schools of Ogemaw County: Volume 1

EDWARDS SCHOOL

1906 - 1907

EDWARDS PUBLIC SCHOOL
District No. 1

Edwards Twp., Ogemaw Co., Mich.

JOHN W. ANGERER, Teacher

Pupils

Grade 1

Ethel Decker
Leo Hepner
Carl Reese
Alex. Gildner
Ethel Decker
Theodore Fournier
Robert Tupper
Glen Miles

Grade 2

Lucy Gildner
Ona Rundel

Grade 3

Gertrude Green
Lawson Cooper
Grace Carpenter
Sadie Griffith
Joseph Rundel
Mame Carpenter

Grade 4

Walter Decker
Lucile Anderson
Nauman Hamilton
Pearl Hill
Gladys Hepner
Clarence Fournier
Belle Tupper

Grade 5

Flossie Decker
Lillie Fournier
Maggie McCauley
Clara Stone
John Gildner
Gale Hepner
Muriel Flint
Jennie McCauley
Warren Williams
Mirinda Sias
Edgar Cooper

Grade 6

May Beckwith
Leo Andrews
Charlotte Williams
Clara Anderson
Orrissi Andrews
Esma Gibson
Chloe Green
Eva Cooper

Grade 8

Clair Decker
Florence Miles
Sammie McCauley
A. J. Ellis
Clyde Brownley

Grade 9

Grace Andersen
Oscar Decker

Review

Maggie Stringer
Fred Loop

School Board

Chas. R. Hamilton - Director
A. H. Flint - Moderator
James Andersen - Treas.

EDWARDS SCHOOL
1907 - 1908

EDWARDS SCHOOL

District No. 1

Edwards Township,
Ogemaw County, Michigan

JOHN W. ANGERER, Teacher

PUPILS

Grade 1
Ethel Decker	Eathel Decker
Theodore Fournier	Robert Tupper
Byron Green	Carl Reese
Glen Miles	Alex Gildner
Wesley Rundell	Grace Buyea

Grade 3
Lucinda Gildner	Ona Rundell
Moses Gerber	David Gerber
Dewey Wallar	

Grade 4
Grace Carpenter	Mame Carpenter
Clarence Fournier	Joseph Rundell
Gertrude Green	Belle Tupper
Pearl Hill	Hazen Wallar

Grade 5
Walter Decker	Lucile Anderson
Blanche Tupper	Flossie Decker

Grade 6
Lillie Fournier	Nauman Hamilton
Warren Williams	John Gildner
Muriel Flint	Charlotte Williams
Jennie McCauley	Maggie McCauley
Clara Stone	

Grade 7
Esma Gibson	May Beckwith
Orrissi Andrews	

Grade 8
Sammie McCauley	Sadie Clayton
A. J. Ellis	Clyde Brownley

Grade 9
Idabel Fournier	Elsie Hollowell
Clair Decker	

Grade 10
Grace Anderson	Oscar Decker

SCHOOL BOARD

Chas. R. Hamilton   A. H. Flint

James Anderson

EDWARDS SCHOOL
1918 - 1919

Muriel Flint (teacher), Kathryn Sergent Harrison, Angie Decker, Gladys Burt Melrose, Thelma Williams Cook, Mamie Decker, Harriett Andrews Husted, Genevieve Bohnard, McKenna Renwick, Florence Andrews Munn, Grace Clayton Beckworth, Rosena Bohnard Fournier, Lucille Decker

Florence Andrews Munn, Genevieve Bohnard Renwick, Harriett Andrews Husted, Clarence Gildner, Ralph Ferguson, Kathryn Sergent Harrison, Angie Decker, Thelma Williams Cook

EDWARDS SCHOOL

From Ogemaw County Herald, October 26, 1939:

EDWARDS SCHOOL

Doesn't time fly fast! Here it is the eighth week of school and we are entering news for the first time this year.

We have three beginners Russell Buckel, Billy Clayton, and Margie Gildner.

We are sorry to hear that Barbara Przylubski is leaving. She is going to attend school in Detroit.

Robert DeMatio is our teacher again this year. We are glad to have him back.

We have a new volley ball. Our teacher has taught us how to play bat ball, kick ball dodge ball and volley ball with it.

Some of the 4-H boys and girls are planning on going to Lansing to the football game on October 28th.

We have organized a book club this year to talk about interesting books. We also plan on some parties and shows.

All of us are working hard to have a good health chart because the winners will be entertained at a Hallowe'en party.

For social science we are making a close study of how the Indians used to live. We have made posters and bows and arrows.

We expect to have many interesting times with Mr. Bray, the recreation leader.

Mr. DeMatio has introduced a new feature this year, which is a daily drill board on such things as Phonics, Arith. Combinations, New Words, Spelling Demons, Important Persons, and Character Traits.

We have our room decorated with witches, black cats, owls, bats, and skeletons for Hallowe'en.

We'll be seeing you again.

Editors —Book club.

EDWARDS SCHOOL
1939 - 1940

Far left:

Floyd Kaiser, Kenneth Barringer, Jay Walter Sergent, DeWayne Tuttle

Next:

Russell Buckel, Joyce Sergent, Ed Buckel, Ronald Sutton, Doris Ruegsegger, Unknown, Paul Clayton

Next:

Bob Buckel, Theodore Fournier, Unknown, unknown Pettifore, Eileen Fournier, Karl Dunn

Next:

Unknown, Earl Bowsher, Phyllis Chapman, Georgina Fournier, Katherine Ruegsegger

Far right:

Clifford Barringer, Junior Fournier, Jean Sergent, Elton Clayton, Donna Sutton, Barbara Palinski, Crandall Sutton

EDWARDS SCHOOL

EDWARDS SCHOOL
1951 - 1952
Kindergarten thru 8th

Top Row:

Mary Jane Nagy, Dale Evilsizer, Sharon Utter, Mike Lantern, Sandra Utter, Butch Bennett, Mona Rhines, Cecil Gildner

Next Row:

Roy Gildner, Catherine Gildner, Norman Pfeiffer, Shirley Prevo, David Gildner, Judy Bennett

Next Row:

Almeda Utter, Gary Sergent, Mary Gildner, Charles Rhines, Joan Oliver, Harold Pfeiffer, Jeanette Gildner, Doug Gildner

Bottom Row:

John Rhines, Phyllis Evilsizer, Edward Poyner, Judy Dunn, Jack Sergent, Ernadine Oliver, Lester Prevo

EDWARDS SCHOOL
1952 - 1953
Beginners thru 8th

Top Row:

Sandra Utter, Mike Lantern, Sharon Utter, Kenneth Bennett, Judy Dunn, Edward Poyner, Judy Bennett, John Rhines

Next Row:

Charles Noel, Mary Gildner, Norman Pfeiffer, Phyllis Evilsizer, Darrell unknown, Marilyn unknown

Next Row:

Catherine Gildner, Doug Gildner, Almeda Utter, Tom Noel, Oka Utter, Harold Pfeiffer, Jeanette Gildner, Dale Evilsizer

Bottom Row:

Gary Sergent, David Gildner, Butch Rhines, Roy Gildner

EDWARDS SCHOOL
1956

Mrs. Kleehammer, Kurt Dunn, Alpha Barley, Carl McCauley, Sue Mackey, Keith McCauley, Linda Poyner, Dick Dunn, Diane Beyerlein (Philbrick), Greg Hacht, Debbie Ehinger (Mier)

EDWARDS SCHOOL
1958 - 1959

Top Row:

Unknown, Donna Spahn, Bill Beyerlein, Diane Beyerlein Philbrick, Carl McCauley, Unknown, Unknown, Unknown, Unknown

Next Row:

Unknown, Audrey Spahn, Unknown, Judy Beyerlein Bernard, Anna Mae Illig, Unknown, Sue Mackey Kleyps, Unknown, Bonnie Dunn

Next Row:

Ronald Ehinger, Kathy Beyerlein Curtis, Dick Dunn, Unknown, Unknown, Unknown

Bottom Row:

Linda Mackey Rowland, Greg Hough Martin, Unknown, Unknown, Linda Poyner Cobb, Keith McCauley, Tom McCauley, Unknown, Sandy Beyerlein Buck

HISTORY OF EDWARDS SCHOOL

By Florence Munn

Reprinted from the *Wilderness Chronicles*

The Edwards School, District #1, Edwards Township, built in 1902, was located on Greenwood Road, one-half mile west of M-30, on property formerly owned by Duff Greenier. Prior to 1902, the first Edwards School Building, Dist. #1, was built about one mile west of the present location on land formerly owned by Mr. and Mrs. Ora Ellis. It was one of four Edwards schools, i.e. the Rau School, corner of Rau road and M-30; the Stillwagon School, corner of Greenwood Road and Stillwagon Road; and the Erb School, corner of Stillwagon Road and Rau Road.

In 1964 the Edwards School and other rural schools were consolidated with the West Branch Public School. Records of some of these schools were stored in the O'Neal School on State Road. This school building burned and records were lost. If there is to be any history of their existence, it will be up to the living to do the remembering and hunt for facts.

The Edwards School was one of the very few schools in Ogemaw County where, at one time, the ninth grade was taught. The O'Neal School taught the ninth grade for a few years, and the North Clemens School in Gladwin County taught the ninth and tenth grades. These schools were quite some distance from a high school and cars were not as yet available. The first year, 1912-1913, that I entered school, in the first grade, the Edwards School was divided into two classrooms. That year, Vera Shrigley taught the older grades, probably the seventh, eighth, and ninth, and Margaret Beemer taught the lower grades. Later Vera Shrigley became the principal of the West Branch High School. Mary (Loop) Loney also taught the older children and later taught many years in the rural schools.

I wish to thank the following Edwards citizens for their contributions, i.e. Mr. Sam McCauley who will be ninety-seven in March, '89 served as a school board member for many years and was a former pupil in the Edwards School when his father, Sam McCauley, Sr. was also a school board member. His wife, the former Helen Wade, still living, was a lifelong resident of the district. Ted Fournier, and his wife, Rosena (Bohnard) Fournier both attended the Edwards School. Ted was in the first grade in 1907. Mrs. Gladys (Hamilton) Mattson's father was a school board member for several years. All of these friends and residents of the Edwards community were very helpful.

A big, big windfall to my hunt for school records came from two of my nieces who live in Bay City, the Mrs. Esther (Ellis) Nussear and the Mrs. Ellen (Ellis) Ralph. Their mother, Orrissi (Andrews) Ellis.... died in 1921. The girls were respectively eight and four years old at the time. Among their mother's cherished possessions left for them, were two school souvenir booklets. One was for the year 1904, and one for the year 1907. There were forty-five pupils in the school year 1903-1904. The picture of the teacher, Olith Tesch, was on the cover. The school board members were: Charles Hamilton, A. H. Flint, and Sam McCauley. In the year 1906-1907 there were fifty-one students. The picture of John Angerer, the teacher, was on the cover. Board members were: Charles Hamilton, A. H. Flint, and James Anderson.

Only one of the souvenir booklets was listed by grade. The following is a complete list of pupils for the 1906-1907 school year. One (*) indicates one who later taught in the Edwards School. Two (**) indicates one who was at some time on the school board. Note: the two names in the first grade list that are identical is not an error. They were twins. One pronounced with the first (E) a long sound, the other with the first (E) a short sound.

HISTORY OF EDWARDS SCHOOL
By Florence Munn

(Continued)

John W. Angerer, teacher. Grade 1; Ethel Decker, Leo Hepner, Carl Reese, Alex Gildner, Ethel Decker, Theodore Fournier, Robert Tupper and Glen Miles. Grade 2; Lucy Gildner and Ona Rundel. Grade 3; Gertrude Green, Lawson Cooper, Grace Carpenter, Sadie Griffith, Joseph Rundel and Mame Carpenter. Grade 4; Walter Decker, Lucille Anderson, Nauman Hamilton, Gladys Hepner, Clarence Fournier and Belle Tupper. Grade 5; Flossie Decker, Lille Fournier, *Maggie McCauley, Clara Stone, John Gildner, Gale Hepner, *Muriel Flint, Jennie McCauley, Warren Williams and Mirinda Sias. Grade 6: May Beck- with, Leo Andrews, Charlotte Williams, Clara Anderson, Orrissi Andrews, Esma Gibson, Chloe Green and Eva Cooper. Grade 8; Clair Decker, Florence Miles, **Sam McCauley, A. J. Ellis and Clyde Brownley. Grade 9; Grace Anderson and Oscar Decker. Review; Maggie Stringer and Fred Loop.

Pupils named in the souvenir book for 1904 that were not named in the 1907 book; Bessie Anderson, Marguerite (Margaret) Beemer, **, Ruth and, Alfred Bernor; Elne Blakely, Clyde Brownley, Bruce, Goldie and Glen Decker, Sadie and Peter Clayton, Ida DeClute, Mamie Fuller, Idabel Fournier, Valentine and Herb Gildner, Florence and Glen Miles, Otis Mutch and Flora St. Johns.

Parents and pupils from 1910 to 1930 who have not been previously named: family name, James Anderson, pupils, Robert, Michael, James and Bessie; Alonzo Andrews, pupils, Harriet, *Florence, Stanley, for a short time a Bobby Ferman (foster child) whose parents died with flu. Dick Alpin, pupils, Devere and Gilmore. Ed Beemer, pupil Ralph Ferguson (foster) a relative. Walter Barringer, pupils, Charlotte and Lucille. Frank Bohnard, pupils, Geneva, Beulah, Rosena and Monroe; Arthur and Mrs. **Brownley, pupils, Mildred, Cyril and Lester. John Clayton, pupils Grace, Carl, Gordon, Helen, Doris, Paul, James, Russel, Arzell, Elton, Bill and Margaret. John Burt, pupils, Ervin, Gladys, John, William and Margaret. ?? Cruckshank, pupils, Lula, Jim, Edna, Gordon, Fred, Roy and Clair. Elmer Decker, pupils, Maime, Elmer, Lucille, Gertrude, Irene (the last of 14 children--because of adverse circumstances, Irene became a foster child in the Charles Hamilton Family from an infant to grown up.) Ora Ellis, (Beatrice and Florence Madden--grandchildren. Jay Ellis, pupil, Esther. Ambrose Flint, ** pupils, Muriel, *Grace Buyeau. Napoleon Fournier, other than mentioned previously, Stanley Walters* (Foster). ?? Galbraith, pupils, Helen and Wesley. Dan Gerber, pupils, Lizzie, Daniel, Amos, Solomon. John Gildner, pupils, Lucinda, Clarence and Alex. Joe Green, pupils, Irene and Joe. Charles Hamilton, pupils, Gladys, Nauman and Irene (foster). ??, pupil, Joseph Rose (foster). Walter Sergent, pupils, Ben, ** and Kathryn. Warren Wade, pupils, Howard Helen, Duane and Clair. Len Williams, pupils, Clair and Alma. Wynotte Williams, pupils, Thelma, Faye and Donald. Fred Williams, pupils, Kathleen, Leota* and Boyd.

A fairly complete list of all teachers in the Edwards School; Mr. ? Paine, Olith Tesch, Mr. Redmond, John Angerer, Alice Williams, Vera Shrigley, Mary (Loop) Loney, Marguerite Beemer (7 years), Maggie McCauley, Muriel Flint, Jesse Shepherd, Florence Munn (5 years), Alice Rabidue, Ada Johnson, Ruth Kleehammer (8 years), Bob DeMatio, Stanley Walters, Anna Mae Riley, Helen Artman, Florence Holt, Leota Williams, Betty Robinson and Marie Buhlman (the last of the Edwards teachers).

HISTORY OF EDWARDS SCHOOL
By Florence Munn

(Continued)

Note: It would be difficult, if not impossible, for me to do justice in naming students who attended Edwards School much later than 1930.

More families from 1910 to 1930: Burt Hamilton family -- Gordon, Orville, Lucille, Mabel, Lorn, Hazel, Rhonda, Lynn, Orthella and Ruby. Later, Orville and Helen (Phillips) Hamilton owned and operated an appliance and furniture store in West Branch. John Stone family -- Clara, Edward -- John Stone was a member of the school board for several years. Sam McCauley family -- Howard -- Later, Howard and Jean (Rutledge) McCauley owned and operated the Whirlpool Appliance Store in West Branch, until retirement. It is still known as McCauley's Appliance. Gus Ewald family -- Joseph Rose (foster). Frank Bohnard family should have read -- Geneva, Beulah, Rosena, Monroe, and Lucille. Alan and Lucille (Bohnard). Frank owned and operated the Dairy Queen in Rose City until retirement. Beulah (Bohnard) Ruegsegger, wife of Sam Ruegsegger, died when their first baby was born. Len Williams family should have read -- Clare, Alma and Clarabelle. Dick and Inez (Cruickshank) Alpin family -- Deverne, Gilmore, Vivian, Don and Bernice. Bernice died when a very young child.

There were four families who had the distinction of having three generations in this school, i.e. the Sam McCauleys, the Warren Wades, the Frank Bohnard and the Tony Ehingers.

The first generation of the McCauley family began with Sam. He was a pupil in 1904, when his father Sam was on the school board. Helen (Wade) McCauley was also a first generation. Howard, son of Sam and Helen, was the second generation, and Howard and Jean McCauley's children, (Carl, Tom, Keith and Connie) were the third generation.

In memory of Sam, the patriarch of the McCauley family: He was a resident of Ogemaw County all his life. He was well-known and well-loved as a neighbor and farmer; had been on the school board many years; he loved and trained horses; was a member of the Edwards Community Church, and a devoted family man. He died April 12, 1989 at the age of ninety-seven. His wife, Helen, still survives.

In the family of Frank and Catherine (Ehinger) Bohnard, there was a Rosena. Ted and Rosena (Bohnard) Fournier were the first generation and both attended the Edwards School.

Their daughter, Eileen (Fournier) Hacht's son Greg, was the third generation of the Frank Bohnard and the Tony Ehinger families. Note: David Hacht was a Michigan State Policeman. He was accidentally killed in a deer hunting accident. Son, Greg, stayed with his grandparents, the Ted Fourniers for several years.

Long before the first printing press; long before there was a paper, or ink, or pens or pencils, our early ancestors carved dates and events in rocks. There has always been a desire to record historical facts for our own gratification and for the benefit of our ancestors.

So let us remember: At least eight students before the year 1930 became teachers. There were five that became merchants.

HISTORY OF EDWARDS SCHOOL
By Florence Munn

(Continued)

Joe Rundel stayed with the Ora Ellis family while in school and later drove a taxi-cab in Bay City Nauman Hamilton completed agricultural courses at Michigan State College (University now). About 1925 and until retirement, A. Jay Ellis worked as a boxcar inspector for the Pere Marquette Railroad in Bay City. Stanley Andrews started to work for the U.S. Postal service at age seventeen. When he retired, he was Assistant Post Master of the West Branch Post Office. Gilmore Alpin, son of Dick and Inez (Cruickshank) Alpin could really play the harmonica. At that time, I'm sure I didn't know what the word "talent" meant. I just knew that he had talent. He should have been in show biz.

Remember when tuberculosis was almost a death sentence? Edna Cruickshank, daughter of James and Ida Cruickshank, when just a young adult, was gravely ill. She had tuberculosis. Her older brothers screened in a part of the porch for a convalescent room at their home. Here she could have the advantage of all the fresh air possible. They gave her the best of care. She did not survive.

Since this was a rural farming community, many stayed on the farm. Some worked on the farm and also worked for a paycheck at other jobs. Many were very successful farmers and would not have wished for any other life.

One of the Edwards farmers was Boyd Williams, son of Fred and Lora (Arrand) Williams. He eventually owned a farm of 328 acres, where he raised both dairy and beef cattle. At one time, this enterprise was considered the third largest in the state. It had two houses, one on land in Edwards Twp., Ogemaw Co. and the other on land in Barrett Twp., Gladwin Co. About 1960, Boyd and hi wife, Arzell (Walker) Williams, left the farm and moved to West Branch. I am not sure if he rented the farm or if he had caretakers.

In West Branch, he eventually owned a gas station and auto parts establishment. He had a wholesale and retail gas and oil business. Some or all of this had been owned by his father-in-law, Fred Walker. While in West Branch, he did alright by himself politically too. He served six years on the West Branch City Council. He served on the Tolfree Hospital Board. He was selected mayor in 1965 and held that position for at least five years. About 1969, he sold the farm to an elderly couple for $90,000; a down payment of $24,000 and yearly payments of $7000. The new owner was paid up in 1971.

It had been Boyd's custom to make occasional visits to his former home place. One day in 1970 he and his five year old grandson made his last visit to this farm. He was shot with a 35 caliber deer rifle. A hearing was held in Gladwin County. William Jennings was the lawyer for the defendent. He had been the lawyer when papers were made for the sale of the land. Because this is such a serious matter and because there are people living who are still grieving over the events of that day, I would choose not to relate other details. If I were to make any comments, it would be with sympathy for all, make any comments, it would be with sympathy for all, and a feeling that this tragedy was the result of a serious life-threatening physical illness, combined with a most significant personality conflict.

The Country Schools of Ogemaw County: Volume 1
HISTORY OF EDWARDS SCHOOL
By Florence Munn

(Continued)

Edwards School personnel after 1930: LeRoy and Marge Barcia (Tom); LeRoy and Marie Bennett (Gerry, Kenneth, Judy); Arnold and Betty Beyerlein (Cathy, Diane, Billy); Rev. Bowditch and Mrs. Bowditch (Marilyn, Donald, Danny); Bob and Mrs. Chapman (Elsie, Peggy, Ruby); Roy and Irene Cruickshank (Billy, Leland); Don and Gerry Dunn (Judy, Bonnie, Dick); Cecil and Maggie McCauley Dunn (Don, Leonard, Doris, Carl); Carl and Ethel Dunn (Carla, Kent); Don and Thelma Evilsizer (Phyllis, Dale, April); August and Georgina Ehinger (Darrel, Ronald, Debbie); Ted and Rosena Bohnard Fournier (Greg Hacht, David Chapman); Clarence and Alvina Fournier (Teresa); Herb and Iva Gildner (Cecil, Roy, Douglas, Margorie, Catherine); Pete and Anna Gerber (Pete); Orie and Bernice King (Bob, Donald); Dan and Fanny Kelsey (Gerry, Delores, Floyd, Leon); Fred and Ruth Klug (Terry, Steve); Ernie and Mrs. Little (Tim, Herb, Mike); J. D. and Kate Mackey (Linda, Sue, Jay), William and Eva Noel (Charles, Tommy, Bobby); Adam and Mrs. Oliver (Max, Ernadene, Joan, Joyce, Alvin); Leonard and Gertie Pfeiffer (Harold, Norman, Harvey); Ed and Jean Poyner (Eddie, Linda); Joe and Mrs. Prevo (Shirley, Lester); Gerald and Shirley Rau (Julie, Jeri); Ben and Clara Rau Sergent (Joyce, Phyllis, Jim, Jack, Gary, Jean, Jay Walter); Leo and Phyllis Spahn (Audrey, Donna); Edward and Mrs. Stone (Eddie Lee, John); Mr. and Viola Tank (Clayton, Beverly); Mr. and Mrs. Timlick (Lila, Betty); John and Mrs. Walls (Max); Wesley and Rose Williams (Bernadene); other children -- parents unknown to me -- Marie Tolfree and Bill Chatterson.

Like any other community, rural or urban, there can be tragedy for some, or triumph for others. Life's successes can be in varying degrees from poverty for some to prosperity for others.

Hopefully, many who remember their school days will have mostly good memories. I had five years with Margaret Beemer as my teacher. It was not surprising that I cherished those years. It is over seventy years ago, but I can remember the noon hour trips to the Duff Greenier woods back of the school; in the spring it was to pick flowers and in the fall to walk through the deep maple and beech leaves; I remember the ten minutes of opening exercises every morning when stories were read or songs were sung. I remember cramming for the seventh and eighth grade exams. We all met in West Branch and Josephine Woods presided over these state exams. Also Josephine Woods visited our school and perhaps told one of Rudyard Kipling's animal stories. One Arbor Day was special. We planted a tree at the corner of the school lot. I think it was an elm. It is there no longer -- perhaps Dutch elm disease took its toll or maybe when the pavement replaced the dirt road more room was needed.

EDWARDS SCHOOL

FOSTER		ROSE	GOODAR
	KLACKING	CUMMING	HILL
OGEMAW	WEST BRANCH	CHURCHILL	LOGAN
EDWARDS	HORTON	MILLS	RICHLAND

EDWARDS ★

ERB SCHOOL

Edwards Township (Town 21 North Range 1 East)

NE 1/4 of SE 1/4 of Section 26 on Stillwagon Road

Began operation in 1889

Built in 1903 by Charles F. Erb on the family property

Consolidated with West Branch Public Schools in 1964

ERB SCHOOL

Teachers:

1925 Lolita Cripps; 1927-28 Marie Ehinger; 1928-1934 Mary Loop Loney; 1934-1936 Julianna Reiter Kube; 1936-1938 Mary Loop Loney; 1938-1939 Joan Wright; 1939-1940 Mary Loop Loney; 1940-1942 Stanley Walter; 1943-1944 Elizabeth Wilcox; 1944-46 Edwin Shiel; 1947-1948 Marjory Mattox; 1948-1950 Veronica Krengielski; 1950-1952 Alice Klann Ohl; 1953-1955 Marie Ehinger Buhlman; 1955-59 Beverly Buhlman; 1959-1963 Leona Holt Cascadden; 1962 Doris Rau (sub for Leona Cascadden); 1963-1964 Kate McLaren <u>Unknown dates:</u> Anna Mae Illig, Thelma Reetz Brick, Elizabeth Buckel, Marie Buckel, Nellie Combs, Olive Yantz, Joanna Rivers, Cameron Sutton (1940-41), Helen Powell, Marie Alenger, Miss Hayes

Students:

Adolph: Elmer, Albert **Bailey:** Josephine, Maxine **Barringer:** Kenneth, Clifford **Bell:** Kenneth **Bowsher:** Earl, Don, Joe **Bray:** George, Jack **Brewer:** Hazel, Kenneth, Arthur, Beatrice, Polly, Joe, Floyd **Buckel:** Russ, Ed, Bob **Burgher:** Clarence, Lois, Ralph, Richard, Lyle **Chapman:** Phyllis **Clayton:** Paul, Elton, Chuck, Jack, Tom, Jim **Crow:** Nina **Curtis:** George, Lee, Leith, Glen Jr., David, Clayton, Virgil, Carl, Dorothy, Mary **Darling:** Vivian **Dunn:** Karl **Eineder:** Nina **Erb:** Bill **Everitt:** Evelyn **Fournier:** Theodore, Eileen, Georgina, Junior **Freeman:** Bobby **Green:** Virginia, Beatrice, Melva, Vern, Tryrus, Frank, Rose Marie **Hanks:** Nancy, Bruce **Hanson:** Elsie, Jane, Gene, George **Illig:** Genevieve, Leo, Norman, Tony, Helen, Floyd, Alfred, Herman, Edward, Irene, James, Leona, Ambrose, Sherman, Adolph, Georgina **Kelsey:** Floyd **Klann:** Tryrus **Knephler:** Marie, Carl **Loney:** Mary **Noel:** Charles, Tom **Moyer:** Jean **Oliver:** Jerry; **Palinski:** Barbara **Pollington:** Viola **Post:** George, Jack, Morden, Milford, Leo, Caroline, Les **Roches:** Pat, Leo, Edwinna **Ruegsegger:** Doris, Katherine **Schaffer:** Frank, Marion, LeRoy, Patty, Sandy **Schmidt:** Murray **Sergent:** Jay, Walter, Joyce, Jean **Sheltrown:** Clyde, Raymond, Jim, Erma, Louise, Eddie, Myrtle, Doreen, Ida Bell, Dorothy, Buster, Ray Jr., Evelyn **Spencer:** Dean **Sutton:** Cameron, Milton, Donna, Ronald, Crandall **Tuttle:** Dewayne **Westwick:** Hazel **Whipple:** Kenneth, Maxine **White:** Mary, Fred, Evelyn, Edward **Zink:** Fred, Junior

ERB SCHOOL

The Erb school was a one story building facing east on Stillwagon Road. A large cast iron stove stood in the corner, which needed wood to burn. It was the boy's job to bring in the wood each morning.

Miss Cripps provided hot lunches to the students until the School Board put a stop to it.

When Cameron Sutton was teaching Erb School, he and the woman he was going to marry took the 7th and 8th grade students on a trip to the Northern Peninsula and the Soo to see geography first-hand.

July 21, 1990: Erb School had a reunion of past students and their spouses. About 30 families came. The teachers who came were: Elizabeth Hewitt Wilcox, Leona Cascadden, Cam Sutton, and Edwin Shiel.

ERB SCHOOL

Wellington R Burt + wife
TO
School District No Three
Edwards Tp, Ogemaw Co Mich.

This Indenture, Made this Fifteenth day of July in the year of our Lord one thousand eight hundred and ~~eighty~~ Ninety four, BETWEEN Wellington R Burt and Annie M. Burt his wife, of the City of Saginaw Michigan, parties of the first part, and The School District Number Three (3) of the Township of Edwards, Ogemaw County, Mich. party of the second part,

WITNESSETH, That the said parties of the first part, for and in consideration of the sum of Twelve #12/100 Dollars, to them in hand paid by the said party of the second part, the receipt whereof is hereby confessed and acknowledged, have granted, bargained, sold, remised, released, aliened and confirmed, and by these presents, do grant, bargain, sell, remise, ~~release~~, alien and confirm unto the said party of the second part, and to its successors ~~heirs~~ and assigns, FOREVER ALL that certain piece or parcel of land, situate lying and being in the _____ of _____ County of Ogemaw and State of Michigan, and described as follows, to wit:

Commencing at the South East Corner of the South East Quarter of the North East Quarter of Section Eight (8) Town Twenty one (21) North, Range one (1) East, running thence West two hundred and two feet (202) ft. thence North two hundred and two (202) feet, thence East two hundred and two (202) feet, thence South two hundred and two (202) feet, to the place of beginning, being one acre of land more or less.

Alexander A. White, Register.

DEED TO ERB SCHOOL LAND
7-15-1894

LIBER ? PAGE ?

Witnesses:
H. M. Prude
Emma S. Burt

Wellington R. Burt (L.S.)
Annie M. Burt (L.S.)

STATE OF MICHIGAN
County of Saginaw ss.
On this Sixteenth day of August in the year one thousand eight hundred and ninety four, before me, a Notary Public in and for said County, personally appeared ~~above~~ named Wellington R. Burt and

ERB SCHOOL
About 1912

ERB SCHOOL
1929

Photo includes:

Lois Burgher Sheck, Arthur Brewer, Hazel Brewer Priddy, Lyle Burgher, Ralph Burgher, Geo. Curtis, Glen Curtis Jr., Leith Curtis, Nina Eineder, Beatrice E. Green Kartes, Virginia Green Schaeffer, Helen Illig, Leo Illig, Sherman Illig, Marie Knepfler Burgher, Geo. Post, Leo Post, Milford Post, Morden Post, Ida Belle Sheltrown, Mary White Sutton.

ERB SCHOOL
1930 - 1931

Back Row:

Floyd Illig, Albert Adolph, Marie Knepfler, Leo Illig, Hazel Brewer, Mary Loney (teacher), Nina Eineder, Erma Sheltrown

Third Row:

Herman Illig, Vivian Darling, Helen Illig, Nina Crow, Art Brewer

Second Row:

Mary White, Milford Post, Ralph Burgher, Genevieve Illig, Beatrice Green, Virginia Green, Edward Illig

Front Row:

Jack Post, Louise Sheltrown, Clarence Burgher, Morton Post, Leith Curtis, Lois Burgher, Jr. (Glen) Curtis, Lyle Burgher, George Curtis, Les Post

ERB SCHOOL
REPORT CARD

PARENTS OR GUARDIANS—PLEASE READ

At the close of each school month, this report is sent to you for inspection. The exact standing of your child is marked X on the report. I hope you will give it the most careful attention and if anything is unsatisfactory inquire of the child for better work or of his interest. It is well to consult the teacher on the marks that are unsatisfactory. The influence of the home and school must work toward the same end; that of doing the greatest good for each child. As a teacher, I shall do all in my power for my pupils, and ask you to frequently visit the school, for your presence would be an inspiration and help to both pupils and teacher.

Mary Loney, *Teacher*

PARENT, PLEASE SIGN BELOW AND RETURN PROMPTLY TO TEACHER

- First Month: Mrs. C. Sheltrown
- Second Month: Mrs. C. Sheltrown
- Third Month: Mrs. C. Sheltrown
- Fourth Month:
- Fifth Month: Mrs. Sheltrown
- Sixth Month:
- Seventh Month: Mrs. C. Sheltrown
- Eighth Month: Mrs. C. Sheltrown
- Ninth Month:

HOME WORK. To Parents—Please report the progress and success in the various divisions here indicated, using letters E, G, M, P, to denote Excellent, Good, Medium or Poor.

PROMOTION CERTIFICATE

This Certifies that Erma Sheltrown has completed grade 7 and is promoted to grade 8.

Mary M. Loney, *Teacher*

TEACHER'S REPORT to PARENTS

"Write it on your heart that every day is the best day in the year."—Emerson

Passed to 8th grade

Ogemaw County, Michigan

- Name: Erma Sheltrown
- District Number: 9
- Grade: 7
- School Year Ending: May 1931
- Teacher: Mary Loney

1—Be
2—Be
3—Be
4—Co
5—Ph

SEVENTH GRADE PUPILS BETTER AVERAGE OF 8TH

Seventh graders in the rural schools of the county made a better showing in their final examinations than the pupils in the rural eighth grades. 76.7 per cent of them passed, it was revealed when announcement of those who were to be promoted was made by the County Board of Examiners.

The announcement showed that out of 107 who took the tests a total of 82 passed and 25 failed. Erma Sheltrown had the highest average with 95 per cent. She is a student of Edwards Dist. No. 8 with Rexford Maas as teacher.

1931

Name: Erma Sheltrown   Grade: 7
Report for year beginning Sept. 1, 1930 and ending May 1931

BRANCHES PURSUED	1st	2d	3d	4th	5th	6th	7th	8th	9th	1st	2d	3d	4th	AVERAGE
READING	B	B	B	C	C	D	B	B		B	C	B		B-
PHYSIOLOGY	C	C	B	C	B	C	A	D	B	B	D			B-
PENMANSHIP	B	B	B	B	B	G	B	B	B					B
ORTHOGRAPHY	S		E	C	C	C	B	E	C	B				C-
MENTAL ARITHMETIC														
HISTORY	C	C	B	C				B						B
GRAMMAR	E	C	D	E	C	C	B	D	B	B				D
GEOGRAPHY	B	B	C	C	C	C	E	D	C	C	D			C-
COMPOSITION														
ARITHMETIC	E	E	D	D	E	C	D	D	D	E	D			D-
DRAWING														
CIVICS														
BOOKKEEPING														
AGRICULTURE														
VISITS OF PARENTS THIS MONTH	0	0	0	0	0	0	0	0						0
BIBLE CREDIT	4	4	4+	4	4	E	E							4+
DEPORTMENT	a	a	a	a	a	a	a	a						a
DAYS PRESENT	14	17	20	13	15	18	17	20	24					162
DAYS ABSENT	4	0	3	4	2	1	0	0						15
TIMES TARDY	0	1	0	0	0	0	1	0						0

GRADE: A 95 to 100 B 85 to 94 C 80 to 85 D 75 to 80 E Below 75

TRAITS of PUPIL

ATTITUDE TOWARD SCHOOL WORK	1st	2nd	3rd	4th	5th	6th	7th	8th	9th
Very Commendable									
Shows Improvement	X	X	X		X	X	X	X	
Gives Up Too Easily									
Copies									
Work Carelessly Done	X				X				
Wastes Time									
Indolent									

RECITATIONS

	1st	2nd	3rd	4th	5th	6th	7th	8th	9th
Very Satisfactory									
Shows Improvement	X	X	X		X	X	X	X	
Inattentive									
Work Shows Falling Off									
Capable of Doing Better	X			X					
Promotion in Danger									
Seldom Does Well									
Appears not to Try									
Comes Poorly Prepared									

CONDUCT

	1st	2nd	3rd	4th	5th	6th	7th	8th	9th
Very Good	X	X	X	X	X	X	X	X	
Shows Improvement									
Restless									
Whispers Too Much									
Annoys Others									
Inclined to Mischief									

ERB SCHOOL

Michigan Public Schools

Certificate of Promotion

This is to certify that __Erma Sheltrown__ of School District No. __3__, of the Township of __Edwards__, County of __Ogemaw__, State of Michigan, has completed the work as outlined in the State Course of Study for the seventh grade and is hereby promoted to the eighth grade.

This certificate should be presented to the conductor at the time of taking the eighth grade examination.

Issued this __4th__ day of __June__, 19__31__

Margaret Husted
County School Examiners

Etta M. Babcock
Commissioner of Schools

_____
Teacher

Office of Commissioner of Schools

West Branch, Mich. June 4, 1931.

Erma Sheltrown

Your standings for Seventh grade examination are as follows:

Orthography and Spelling	90
Writing	95
Reading	100
Physiology	95
Geography	95

An average of 75 percent and a minimum of 60 is required.

Seventh grade pupils who fail to reach an average of 75% and a minimum of 60 in all subjects may take the eighth grade next year providing they obtain a grade of at least 75 in each of a majority of the subjects. Such pupils will be required to take subjects in which they fail with the eighth grade next year.

Seventh grade standings MUST be kept and shown to teacher at the beginning of school next year before pupils are admitted to eighth grade.

Etta M. Babcock
Commissioner.

Passed

ERB SCHOOL
1931 - 1932

Back Row:

Mary Loney (teacher), Leo Illig

Next Row:

Evelyne Sheltrown, Kenny Bell, George Curtis, Lois Burgher, Beatrice Green, Genevieve Illig, Morden Post, Elsie Hanson, Helen Illig, Herman Illig, Clarence Burgher, Mary White

Next Row:

Dorothy Curtis, Caroline Post, Leona Illig, Melva Green, Donna Sutton, Crandall Sutton, Ambrose Illig, Jane Hanson, Frank Green, Junior Zink, Earl Bowsher, Richard Burgher

Front Row:

Don Bowsher, Joe Bowsher, Ed Illig, Glen Curtis (Jr.), George Hanson, Leith Curtis, Raymond Sheltrown, Ralph Burgher, Milford Post, Jack Post

ERB SCHOOL

Public School Diploma

Ogemaw County
Michigan

This certifies that _John C. Post_ is a graduate of _Erb School, Dist. No 3_ and has completed the studies prescribed for the first eight grades of the Public Schools of Michigan and is therefore awarded this

Diploma

Given in Ogemaw County, _May 16_ 193_7_

Mary M. Loney, TEACHER

Delia B. Neal, COUNTY COMMISSIONER OF SCHOOLS

ERB SCHOOL

Ogemaw County Herald, October, 1938:

ERB SCHOOL NEWS

Our school windows are decorated with cats and pumpkins. We are busy decorating the black boards with leaves.

The seventh and eighth grades are making Current Event books.

Erb school 24, Stillwagon school 12 was the score in the soft ball game at the Stillwagon school Friday, October 7.

We are sending for our geography note books. We are very anxious to get them.

We are very grateful to the school board for building us a book shelf.

We wish to thank Miss Campbell for bringing out the books loaned by the Children's Fund of Michigan.

We are saving the copies of Michigan My Michigan that appear in the Bay City Times.

We have joined the Automobile Club of Michigan again this year with the same captain, Jr. Curtis.

The seventh and eighth grades are studying about the coming of the Pilgrims in history.

The third grade is studying about the cave people in geography.

Some of us attended the Music Meet Wednesday.

We have our light fixtures but not electricity. We hope it will get here soon.

Our 4-H Club is to organize with 9 in handicraft and 5 in sewing projects.

We have 29 pupils in school this year including 2 beginners.

The beginners and first grade are making number books.

Ronald Sutton is wearing glasses this year.

We have new brooms, erasers and coal pail.

The Misses Carr of Grayling visited the Erb school Monday, October 17.

We are planning a box social for Friday, Oct. 28. Proceeds are to be used for a trip to the Royal Oak Zoo. Women please bring boxes, men don't forget your pocket books.

ERB SCHOOL
1944

List of Students:

Josephine Bailey, Maxine Bailey, Carl Curtis, Clayton Curtis, Virgil Curtis, Tryrus Green, Vern Green, Bruce Hanks, Nancy Hanks, Georgina Illig, Irene Illig, James Illig, Tryus Klann, Carl Knepfler, Jerry Oliver, Edward White, Evelyn White, Fred White, Don unknown

ERB SCHOOL

By Hazel LaDonna Brewer Priddy

(Reprinted from "The Erb Family History" by William Erb, who lived in Oscoda, now living in Flint)

The Erb School was built in 1903 by Charles F. Erb with the help of a "work bee" comprised of neighbors and other members of the Erb family. The lumber, undoubtedly, was supplied from trees on the Erb property that were processed thru Samuel Erb's saw mill. This saw mill was located near Christopher Erb's "house of seven gables" on Stillwagon Road just south of the school.

It was built on an acre of land 202 feet by 202 feet that was located in the SE corner of the SE 1/4 of the NE 1/4 of Section 8 in Edwards Township, Ogemaw County, Michigan. The site is located about 1/2 mile North of Lehman Road on the west side of Stillwagon Road.

School District Three, Edwards Township, bought this property from Wellington R. and Annine M. Burt of Saginaw, Michigan on July 15, 1894 for $12.00.

This property abuts land owned by the White family who unknowingly paid taxes on it for years.

The building was a one story, rectangular, frame structure with a cut field stone foundation and crawl space under it. It faced East on Stillwagon Road. There was a boy's coatroom on the left as you entered and the girl's coatroom on the right. The floors were hard wood. A large cast iron wood stove sat in the north-west corner of the building. It was moved to the NE corner in the 30's. A metal jacket was installed around the stove later and finally it was replaced by a oil circulator stove.

The school board paid to have wood and pine stumps supplied for the winter. The boys brought the wood from the wood shed at the rear of the building into the wood box by the stove.

There were outside toilets for both the boys and the girls that were tip-over targets during Halloween. Sometime in the late twenties toilets were installed in each coat room. These required water to flush them that had to be carried from the hand pump near the front of the building. They "flushed" into a pit. The water had to be carried from a neighbor's well before the school got its own well. In the late 30's when electricity was available the neighbors had a work bee to install a septic tank and field. The well was hooked up to an electric pump.

Sometime prior to 1923 the building was veneered with a salmon colored brick. In the early 1930s, most of the windows on the North side were moved to the South side and the openings on the North side were bricked in to conserve heat in the winter.

On January 21, 1980 the property was sold by sealed bid to M. C. Rau for $2,425.10. Mr. Rau's wife Evelyn (White) had her brother Fred M. White tear it down shortly after they bought it. Some of the bricks were given to a church while the bell and "1903" date stone were retained by Fred White.

I remember one Christmas my brother, Arthur, caught a mink and sold the hide and bought a new suit for the Christmas program.

We had a big stove that I believe was heated with coal. After I was out of school and my brothers had one more year to go they installed inside toilets in the school. This was about 1930.

One time when my sister was going there one of the sons of the Fermens who had died from the flu, committed suicide. He was living with Mr. Frank Adolph not far from the Erb place when he shot himself in the woods on the hill. He had become so lonely for his parents

ERB SCHOOL
By Hazel Priddy

(Reprinted from "The Erb Family History" by William Erb, who lived in Oscoda, now living in Flint)

(continued)

My sister and the teacher got all the kids from the Erb School to go and see him laid out in his overhauls. He was about 15 years old.

I don't remember too much about the teachers punishing the kids. However, back in 1929 we had a young teacher from Normal who couldn't make some of the big boys in the Erb School mind. She left in December when I was in the sixth or seventh grade and we got a mean teacher to replace her. I got along with her and the kids knew they had to settle down which they did.

When we were in the 8th grade in May we had to go to West Branch High School for the 8th grade exams. This was hard on us because we didn't get to West Branch very much and we weren't use to the school either. If you passed you could go on to high school. But if you failed you had to go back to grade school. However, if you failed and were sixteen years old you didn't have to go back.

When I was in the seventh grade I remember reading a book about two boys who were trappers way up north at Ontonagon in the upper peninsula. I had a test on that book, it was so interesting that I still remember it.

They started the Union Sunday School at the Erb School in 1928 and had bible school in the summer. I had big feet and the neighbors would kid me about them. I made out an order for new shoes to Sears and sent it to the school to catch the mailman. Then I worried over the mailman looking at the order and seeing the size of my feet. I was so proud of the shoes when they came that I put them on and walked that 1-1/2 miles thru the fields to Sunday school. They were too narrow and I got bunions on my feet so I walked home bare footed. I still have those bunions.

I got married on Christmas evening and for entertainment we took in the Christmas programs at the Erb School as well as programs at the Rau and Stillwagon Schools.

Norman Illig, born in 1910, and his brother, Tony born in 1912, live on Lehman Road just East of Stillwagon Road. They said that "they went to the Erb School all our lives". Their grandfather homesteaded on Rau Road in the late 1890's. They remember that the teacher use to discipline the students "by slapping their hands with a ruler". However, if the student was very bad, "the teacher made the student sit under her desk."

When the Ogemaw Schools consolidated in 1965, Genevieve Kloberg was instructed to deliver the "Erb School" board minutes to the old high school. The officials there said they took them to the new high school

I spent 2-1/2 hours searching for these records at the new high school to no avail. I am sure that these records were not destroyed. It is a shame that these school board records are not available to review because they contain a wonderful record of life in the early Edwards Township.

The teachers I remember were, Nellie Combs, Marie Ehinger, Mary Loney and Mrs. Harry Buckel. I worked for the Erb School for two years carrying in wood and taking care of the fire and received $5.00 a month. In the winter months we took turns bringing meat and vegetables to school to make bean soup or stew so we all could have a bowl of hot soup at noon.

ERB SCHOOL
By Hazel Priddy

(Reprinted from "The Erb Family History" by William Erb, who lived in Oscoda, now living in Flint)

(continued)

We would practice our Christmas play for about two weeks so we could recite it for our parents some night before Christmas. I can remember going to the play riding in a horse drawn sleigh and covered up with blankets. We lived on Rau Road 1-3/4 miles from the school.

We used to play ball against the Rau, Stillwagon and Edwards Schools. The big deal was to hit the ball across the road at the Erb School.

In the spring we had a big picnic for the families. Sometimes we hated to see the last day of school because it meant that we had to start work on the farm.

I did not attend the school as a student. In fact, I was in the 11th grade in high school when my family moved to Edwards Twp. I graduated from high school in June, 1934, and did not attend County Norman until the school year of 1940-41. This entitled me to a three year teaching certificate. I taught for one year at the Erb School, Sept. 1941 until June 1942. I had all eight grades and I believe there were 37 students.

School was scheduled to start on a Monday morning. Four days before school started, a neighbor friend and I decided to take a trip around Lake Michigan. On Sunday morning, we were somewhere in Wisconsin, and we took turns driving (changing every half hour) and arrived at 3:00 a.m. Monday morning. Naturally, I was rather tired and hurting from lack of sleep. I arrived at the school about 8:00 a.m., greeted the children, distributed the test books, assigned some lessons, and dismissed all students at 11:30 a.m. (Just as though it was always done this way).

The desk in the school (for the teacher) was like a table with the legs and open under the top. I had one girl who liked to visit with her neighboring students, so I asked her to come up and sit under the desk as a form of discipline. I carried my lunch in old fashion lunch box and usually put it by my feet, under the desk. This girl opened my lunch box and ate all my lunch all the time I'm wondering why the rest of the room thought it was so funny that this girl had to sit under the desk.

I had started to wear glasses (spectacles) for reading, and occasionally removed them. One day as I removed the glasses, one of the students whispered to those around her. Naturally, I spoke up and suggested that she tell everyone in the room what she had said. The student (happened to be a younger sister of Mary's) said. "I just told that you don't look any smarter than anyone else when you take your glasses off."

For a special program at Halloween, we scheduled an old fashioned box social and invited all the parents. This was the first time I had encountered many of the parents. I made a little speech, inviting any parent to stop in and discuss any problems they had with the teaching program, their children, etc. I had rented a movie projector and a Fox Movietone film from a camera store in town. When I started to show the film it was not rewound and it was starting from the end of the film. I was a trifle upset and ad-libbed for a bit while I removed the film and started it over from the beginning. This time I had the film in backwards, like looking at the reverse of a negative. Finally I got things straightened out and we enjoyed the movie.

ERB SCHOOL
By Hazel Priddy

(Reprinted from "The Erb Family History" by William Erb, who lived in Oscoda, now living in Flint)

(continued)

The rural school Christmas program is always a highlight, both with the students and with the parents. The students miss a lot of studying. We planned quite an extensive program, contests between the fathers and the mothers in the audience and as an added feature had one of the parents sit behind the curtain and play a guitar while three girls (students) stood in front of the curtain and sang. One of the girls was holding a guitar and faking playing. I overheard some remarks from some of the mothers in the audience that she didn't approve of her daughter taking guitar lessons instead of studying more scholastic types of endeavor. We had rehearsed three songs and the hoax was not discovered until the girls were asked to do several encores. Without having practiced these additional songs, the guitar player behind the curtain started playing before the girl in front got her instrument in position to play. These gave our secret away and everyone got a big chuckle from it.

The road from White's corner to Curtis' farm occasionally got plugged with snow drifts and for one four week period that winter it was not plowed. I stayed with John and Hattie Fick for 4 weeks and walked to and from the school. I remember that I had to climb up an old fashioned ladder (nailed to the wall) to get to my sleeping quarters, a loft above Fisk's living quarters.

We decided to build a couple of basketball backboards and install baskets for the playground. I allowed some of the older boys (during school hours) to get a couple of old telephone poles along the road going to Tee Lake. One of the area residents (Elmer Adolph, he's dead now, so I'll mention his name) tried to run the boys off. The boys got really sassy and neglected to tell me when they came back with the poles. Later, that same day, Mr. Adolph stormed into the school, shouting that he didn't approve of my teaching the students to steal, etc. He even invited me outside to do battle with him. I remember some of the girls crying as I went outside with Mr. Adolph. We had quite a discussion, but no fisticuffs. Later that same year, all the rural teachers were asked to register everyone in the district for sugar rationing. I had everyone in the area registered except the Adolph family. On the last day for registering, about five minutes before I was ready to lock the school and head for home, Mr. Adolph showed up to register. Incidentally, after four years of military service during 1942-46, I started working for a petroleum dealer in
W.B. and Mr. Adolph always purchased his fuel from this dealer. There were four people in the office and unless he could talk to me, he would not leave an order or pay his account.

At the end of the school year, I asked the parents of the 7th and 8th graders (3 girls and 2 boys) if I could take these five students on a 3 day trip. We went to the Upper Peninsula and on to Sault Ste. Marie, spent some time at the lock, etc. Mary and I were not married at that time and I suggested that she accompany us, sort of a chaperon for the girls. Some mothers were outraged at the suggestion but Mrs. Hanson, (bless her heart) convinced the others that it would be okay.

After several months of "teaching" I found that I was "testing" the students on their daily assignments. I learned to teach. I would give an assignment, and then the class, with my assistance would prepare a set of questions (where, what, when, why, who, etc.) for which they could determine the answers in doing their homework.

Ogemaw County Genealogical & Historical Society

ERB SCHOOL

By Hazel Priddy

(Reprinted from "The Erb Family History" by William Erb, who lived in Oscoda, now living in Flint)

(continued)

South from the corner of Rau and Stillwagon Roads: Traveling along a narrow road, we find that high banks on each side formed a natural receptacle for heavy snows which occurred often in the mid nineteen thirties. Erb, a one room brick school stands on the right side of the road, atop a small hill. Resting on a one acre plot, this was the social and political center of the North Edwards community. The school provided a good learning opportunity. Reading, writing and arithmetic, were the basic subjects. Other subjects included: spelling, penmanship, geography, history, music and art. Each child was assigned one of the stationary desks, containing a book storage space, a pencil and pen grove and an ink well.

On a rigid fifteen minute modular schedule, "grades" were summoned forward to the "recitation row", for "Class." Those students not in "class" continued their studies and on occasion, became involved in "Horse Play". The system provided a natural review and reinforcement process as students listened.

The success of the school depended on the skill of the teacher. Most elementary school teachers had attained less than two years of training beyond High School. County Normal schools were the primary training laboratories. These schools, usually housed in the High School building furnished most of the training for one room school teachers.

Recess, my favorite time, was often occupied by ball games, with the teacher as a participant.

The one room school became a learning laboratory for eight years each for the ten Curtis kids. Schools of the county received general supervision from the elected County School Commissioner. An elected Board administered the Erb School. My dad served as one of three members on the Erb school board. Others who served included Ray Sheltrown, Chris Crow and Frank Green. I remember several teachers of that era including Mary Loney, Juanita Reiter, Nellie Combs and Mrs. Yantz. Teachers often earned extra pay for doing the janitorial work.

Parents were often involved in school events. Christmas programs provided an opportunity for children to demonstrate their skills with recitations, songs and skits. Box Socials, with ladies preparing decorated packages of goodies for sale, were popular.

The highest bidder on each box earned the honor of dining on the contents with the fair lady donor. Men often pilfered the secret of ownership of a particular box then bid vigorously against a friend as he attempted to purchase a particular box. A variation was a Shadow Box to social. Bidding took place as the lady stood behind a curtain, creating a shadow profile, while her box was auctioned.

I remember: skating on the pond, spelling contests with other schools, baseball games, carrying water some distance when the well went dry, visits from the commissioner and eight grade exams to determine passing certification of completion of required schooling. Failure to pass required continued attendance until age sixteen.

I started school when I was seven years old. Had to walk, alone, until I got to the Adolph farm. Sometimes I'd be in time to walk with Elmer and Albert, or maybe the Brewer children. Adolphs lived on the

ERB SCHOOL
By Hazel Priddy

(Reprinted from "The Erb Family History" by William Erb, who lived in Oscoda, now living in Flint)

(continued)

same road as I did, to the east of Dads farm and the Brewers lived on the west side of Tee Lake. They were Beatrice, Polly, Joe, Art and Hazel. At times we'd go from Adolphs, across the fields and woods but other times we had to walk the roads to the corner where the Curtis family lived.

My first teacher was Mary (Mrs. James) Loney. It was 1st grade, no pre start or kindergarten then. When I was real young I'd always cry whenever Mamma showed anyone my "first-day-of-school" picture. I looked so SAD! Mrs. Loney had already been my parents teacher (when I don't know) and I was scared of her. She was strict and a darn good teacher. The best one I ever had! After first grade I had Leatha Cripps for 2 years, then Marie Ehinger. Miss Cripps was fat and soft like a marshmallow, Mrs. Ehinger was young and slim and pretty. She wore black patent leather high heeled pumps at school! She was "fashionable", young, we all liked her. Before that when Miss Cripps was teaching we had a tragedy. An 8th grader, Bobby Freeman shot himself. Harold or "Hutch" came to the school and told Miss Cripps. She really cried so hard. School was dismissed right away. When I was in 2nd or 3rd grade, my sister Louise started school there, too. Mamma packed us such big lunches, we always had a picnic (in nice weather) with the Adolph and Brewer kids under a favorite shade tree between the Curtis farm and Adolphs, where Brewers cut through the Windover farm. Adolphs were home and Louise (now L. Bennett) would continue west about a half mile. One of the teachers almost was "fired" or was threatened to be one beautiful spring day. Must have been 80 so we all took our lunches and went on a "field trip" for the afternoon, instead of classes. What a terrible thing to do and all us kids thought it was a terrific day! The Illig kids east of Curtis farm used to gather and eat leeks every spring and would get sent home because they really did "stink." I still like them even tho they are worse than garlic for odor.

The Illigs were German and the kids spoke German, at times, at school. They made life miserable for Hazel Brewer (Priddy now) and me. She had long straight hair, in two fat braids and I had long curls, the kind that mamma wrapped around her finger. They'd chase us and pull our hair. We were terrified (no big brothers would whip that many "Dutch men") but one day I put an end to it. Our teacher (and my folks) said we had to fight our own battles after we left school. So, one day Leo Illig chased us up a road bank and I hit him in the head with my dinner bucket, still half full of lunch, he rolled down to the road and was stunned for a few seconds. He hasn't forgotten it yet and he mentions it about every time I see him every year or so, usually at funerals! From that day on, Hazel and I walked in peace the half mile before we went west and they went east.

Mrs. Loney's husband Jim always drove her to school. They lived a mile or so South in Clements township. (I think) east of the Stillwagon school. Can't say for sure, now, but I think Miss Cripps boarded with my Dad's Uncle Harry and Aunt Annie White, 1/2 mile north of the school. Miss Ehinger boarded with Helen and Bill Burger (Helen Curtis). That was a mile from school. Sometimes we'd get to school before the "teacher" did, fun when it was nice but terrible on cold weather. We had a huge round furnace in the SE corner of this one room and waited for teacher to build fire. Had outside "john", naturally way to the back of the school yard. Nasty boys would hang around and try to "peek" thru cracks! And those same kids would try to "tickle our palms" and laugh like crazy and talk German and we knew it was something "dirty". At times in the winter our water pump would be frozen

ERB SCHOOL

By Hazel Priddy

(Reprinted from "The Erb Family History" by William Erb, who lived in Oscoda, now living in Flint)

(continued)

so the older boys would go 3-4 city blocks to the nearest farm to bring drinking water back. Mattie Sinn and John Fick's (they weren't married!!) Can't recall now, but one day one of those rotten boys "peed" in it. He confessed to the teacher but after half of us had tried to drink it. Don't remember any more about that incident!

We had fun there too. Every year a x-mas program, last day of school was really special .New dress and huge family picnic. We went to Tee Lake some but May 15-18th isn't really swimming weather but some tried it anyway.

In the winter we had a skating party right down the S. hill from the school. Some had sleds we could take to school, don't remember any one with real bought skates. Couldn't go over the fences when there was water there.

I saw lots of old school records there but one of the teachers, Mr. C. or Miss Ehinger cleaned out all the old book shelves one day and burned them so the school board was up in arms again. Saw my Dad's and his three brother's records. They were Clyde, Ray and Jim Sheltrown. Uncle Clyde lived for a few years on a land-locked "40" just west of the school. Uncle Clyde's kids, Eddie Myrtle and Doren (deceased) went to Erb, later a couple of Uncle Jim's kids, Idabel (deceased) and Jimmie and still later Uncle Ray's kids, Dorothy (deceased), Buster (Ray Jr.) and Evelyn. The Post kids George and Leo and Jack were with us, Marie (Knephler) Burgher. Some of Bill and Helen's kids, Lyle and Lois and a couple of younger ones, Nina and Murry Smith, and we had the Roches too, Pat and Leo and Edwina. Pat and Edwina both gone now, so is Art Brewer, but Joe still lives on Tee Lake.

One of our teachers, Miss Cripps, used to make (a) big kettle of creamed potatoes, soups and she even had fried rabbit the older boys brought. Finally the school board members put a stop to the hot lunches too!

Ole "Link" lived on E. side of road before Curtis' corner, across from the big unfinished house. Some- one lived there in 2-3-4 rooms, seems like it was a woman. Later Eineder's, Jay and Jennie and daughter Nina lived there and a son Robert (retarded). They also lived awhile where Posts' lived, 1-1/4 miles west of Uncle Harry Whites and after the Posts moved to Fredrick.

I will try to write you some of my recollections of the time I attended Erb School, but I want you to be aware that my memory is dim and I only attended the school from the first grade through the fourth at the ages of six through nine. I am now sixty seven.

I lived with my grandparents, Harry and Anna White, my Aunt Matie and my Uncle Fred. (They are brother and sister; neither had ever married) There was a hired man who lived with us whose name is Chris Crow and I thought a lot of him. He was like a member of the family.

My parents, Harry and Marjorie (Priddy) White and my brothers and sisters lived in Bay City where my father was a railway mail clerk on the Pere Marquette railroad.

I rejoined my family in Bay City and graduated from Central High School in June, 1941. In fact, on

ERB SCHOOL
By Hazel Priddy

(Reprinted from "The Erb Family History" by William Erb, who lived in Oscoda, now living in Flint)

(continued)

June 15th, I will attend our 50th class reunion.

That's my background and now for some recollections of my time spent at Erb School.

I remember it as being a happy time and I was contented in living on the farm. There are two teachers that "stand out" in my memory -- Nellie Combs and Mary Loney.

Mary Loney was my teacher for most of the time I attended Erb. She was a very strict teacher, but a good one. I credit her with my getting a good start, and also, being a good reader. There were times when I provoked her with my whispering, etc., because I remember on one occasion that she pulled me up out of my seat and ripped a button off my shirt! Needless to say, I deserved it. She was always fair. We knew when she was getting angry because her neck would start getting red and the redness would slowly creep up to her face.

The Christmas programs were always an exciting time! I was a quick learner and by the time the program was presented to the parents and others, I had memorized everyone's recitation and part in addition to my own.

Nellie Combs was a teacher before Mary Loney and the reason I remember her is because she gave me a little book titled "Peter Rabbit" for being the best behaved pupil in the school! She didn't teach very long because the "older and big" boys were too difficult for her to handle. I won't mention them by name here!

The games we played mostly were tag, hide and seek, and fox and geese. There was a pond below the school to the south and in the winter when it was frozen, we played on it.

I walked to school because my grandparents lived only half a mile from it. Sometimes, I would "cut through" the field instead of walking around by the road. Sometimes these walks home from school involved petty arguments and fights among several of the kids. I never got seriously involved in any of the snowball or stone-throwing but I remember being very upset when Kenneth Bell would hang my lunch box up in a tree too high for me to reach!

I may have been a little luckier that most of my classmates because I always had a good lunch to carry and nice clothes to wear. I remember some of the pupils being barefoot in school and sandwiches brought of bear meat and of brown sugar and sour cream.

Several of the boys sitting on the ground in one of the school pictures are barefoot.

Of course, there were also the "romances!" (ha) I wrote my share of love notes (and sometimes Mary Loney intercepted them!) It was always a sad affair when my "romance of the moment" turned his attentions to another!

ERB SCHOOL & MARY LONEY

By Genevieve Illig Kolberg & Leo Illig

(Reprinted from "The Erb Family History" by William Erb, who lived in Oscoda, now living in Flint)

Leo Illig was born in Edwards Township in 1918. His sister Genevieve Illig Kolberg was born there in 1922. Their father was two years old when his family came to Edwards Township from Formosa, Canada in wagons. They would place logs under the wagon to float them across the rivers. Their father and grandfather lumbered in Edwards Township. Their father went to the Rau School thru the second grade.

Leo was under the impression that Charlie Erb built the Erb School. They remember that the county officials had bricked up the window of the school on the north side to conserve heat. There was a hand water pump near the front of the school. Before they got the pump they had to carry water from neighbor John Grigg's place. The school yard was fenced in. No one had to cut the grass because the kids kept the grass trampled down.

In the winter they would get permission from their parents to go over the fence and slide down the hill to the frozen pond next to the school. This land belonged to Cyrus Erb in the early 1900's. The boys would play hockey on the pond.

They lived on Lehman Road and walked to school. Their lunch pails would sometimes contain syrup and bread or bean sandwiches. Once in a while they would trade their lunch for someone else's lunch.

The school was heated by a cast iron stove that sat in the northwest corner of the building when Leo went there. Later, while Genevieve attended the school, they had placed a metal jacket around the stove. It had a door that opened onto a shelf ahead of the fire pot. In the winter the mothers would take turns bringing pails of soup for the kids. They would heat the soup on this shelf. They would burn pine stumps in the stove. Later on they had a fuel oil heater. Sometimes it would be so cold the kids never took their coats off.

The floor of the school was hardwood. The school board would hire women to scrub it and mop oil over it. The school got electricity in 1930 so they installed lights hanging from the ceiling. They installed toilets in the boy's and girl's coatroom that were over pits dug under the school. The kids had to carry pails of water to flush them. Later the men had a work bee to install septic tanks and inside water.

They had desks that sat two or three students. Later each student had their own desk. The desks had ink wells. They used the straight ink pens with removable points. They would buy "Big Ben" tablets. When they first got pencils with removable erasers Clarence Berger was showing his classmates how to pull off the eraser and blinded one of his eyes with the point of the pencil. Genevieve remembers having good teachers: Elizabeth Buckle, Joana River and Marie Alanger. The teacher she and Leo remember most of all was Mary Loney.

MARY LONEY: Mary Loney started teaching in Edwards Township in 1928. She would alternate between the Stillwagon and Erb Schools. She was a hard teacher and very strong. She was there to teach and wouldn't put up with nonsense. If you acted up she would hit you over the head with anything she had in her hand at that time. Lee Curtis was sent to the blackboard to do an arithmetic

ERB SCHOOL & MARY LONEY

By Genevieve Illig Kolberg & Leo Illig

(Reprinted from "The Erb Family History" by William Erb, who lived in Oscoda, now living in Flint)

(continued)

problem. He started fooling around so she hit him over the head with a broom handle and knocked him out. His mother came the next day and told her it's okay to punish Lee but don't hit him on the head.

Leo Illig weighed 150-160 pounds when he went to school. This didn't stop Mary Loney. She would pick him up off the floor. When his mother asked why his shirt buttons were torn off he told her "Mary did it". When she gave a test on verbs and adverbs she told Genevieve Illig that she must have cheated because she got so many right. So she sat Genevieve at her desk and made her retake the test. This time she got even more correct and again passed the test. Mary Loney never apologized. Genevieve was good on math bees and her sister was too in spelling bees.

Mary Loney was a hard teacher but she was also fair. She was going to make those kids learn. The school had 35-40 students from the first grade thru the eighth grade. In addition she had a kindergarten class and special learning students. She earned $35.00 a month plus $5.00 a month to have the fire going and the floors swept before the kids got there in the morning.

Both Leo and Genevieve feel a one-room school was the best place for learning because the older kids helped teach the younger ones. Mary Loney never quit teaching her students even after they had left school. Genevieve remembers meeting Mary shortly before Genevieve was to start work in a store in West Branch. This was in 1947. Mary took her home, got out a box of play money, and was going to teach her how to make change.

Leo and Genevieve remembered the excitement of Christmas at the Erb School. They would practice the play, make stage props and curtains. The costumes were made from old sheets. The angel wings were cardboard and painted. They would cut and twist red crepe paper for tree decorations. Strings of popcorn would finish the tree. They never bought decorations nor were there any lights on the tree. They would draw names and exchange gifts like pens and pencils. Someone had donated an organ to the school so they had music and sang carols.

Genevieve and some of the mothers founded the "Mother's Club" whose purpose was to help the school. One Valentine they surprised the kids and the teacher by walking into the school with food for a Valentine party.

Genevieve served ten years on the Erb School board until the schools were consolidated in 1965.

ERB SCHOOL
1951-1952
Kindergarten thru 8th

Top Row:

Alice Klann (teacher), Frankie Schaffer, Mary Curtis, David Curtis, Marion Schaffer

Middle Row:

Adolph Illig, Charlie Noel

Bottom Row:

Tom Noel, Jim Clayton, Rose Marie Green, Jack Clayton, Chuck Clayton

ERB SCHOOL REUNION

Ogemaw County Herald
July 27, 1989

Rural school reunion

Sixty-five students and teachers of Ogemaw County schools met for their annual reunion at Logan Township Hall, July 15. Emma Thorne presided over the business meeting. New officers were elected: Don Smith, president; Frank Bennett, vice president; Betty Weaver and Correan Clemens Meir, secretary and treasurer. Teachers attending the reunion included Ann Quigley, Wilma Quigley, Beulah Gallagher, Emma Thorne, and Verba Miracle. Students from 13 different schools were present, including 13 from Red School, 11 from O'Neil, nine from Palmer, five each from Atherton and Campbell Corners, four from Rifle River, three from Withey, two each from Nester, Stanlake and O'Connor, and one each from Eastside and Evergreen. Door prizes were won by Lorna Middleton, Ester Quigley, and Vern Benjamin. Theo Beach traveled the farthest from Yuma, Ariz. Leita Ferguson was the oldest present, and Rolland Benjamin the youngest who attended a rural school. Don Smith was the auctioneer.

ERB SCHOOL REUNION

July 21, 1990

Attendees:

Jack Post, Milford Post & wife, George Curtis & wife, Leith Curtis & wife, Glen Curtis Jr., David Curtis & wife, Genevieve (Illig) Kolberg, Leo Illig, Helen (Illig?), Beatrice (Green) Kartes & husband, Melva (Green) Goldy & husband, Milton Sutton, Donna (Sutton) Neubecker & husband, Josephine (Bailey) Neubecker & husband, George Bray & wife, Jack Bray & wife, Kenneth Whipple, Maxine (Whipple) & husband, Lois (Burgher) Sheick & husband, Ralph Burgher & wife, Elsie (Hanson) Noffsinger, Kenneth Bell & wife, Marie (Knephler) Burgher, Carl Knephler, Hazel (Brewer) Priddy & brother, Joe Brewer, Murray Schmidt & wife, Louise (Sheltrown) Bennett, Fred White & wife, and Mary & Cam Sutton.

Teachers who were there:

Elizabeth (Hewitt) Wilcox, Leona Cascadden, Cam Sutton.

Edwin Shiel, Stanley Walters and Helen Howell weren't there but Helen Howell did correspond from Florida.

EVERGREEN SCHOOL

(Originally named Peters School)

Klacking Township (Town 23 North Range 2 East)

NW ¼ of SW ¼ of Section 12 on Campbell Road

Teachers:

1901-02 Alta Goff; 1903-04 Olive Janson; 1910-11 E. Florence Nolan; 1913 Lottie Chambers Meadows; 1916-17 Alice Rabidue; 1918-1919 Belle Bixby Trainor; 1919-1920 Anna McLees; 1920-21 Eleanore Bixby; 1921-23 Verba Chase; 1923-25 Cordie Rusher; 1924-26 Hiram Rose; 1926-27 Gladys Reetz Rice; 1927-28 Pearl Rose Mason; 1928-29 Viola Schick; 1930-31 Marie Buhlman; 1934-36 Julianna Reiter Kube; 1936-37 Mary Loop Loney; 1937-38 Theresa Slater; 1940-41 Leona Moyer; 1941-43 Arlene Grawburg; 1946-47 Leona Moyer; 1947 (Sept-Dec. sub) Joan Green; 1948 Leona Moyer; 1948-49 Joan Green; 1949-50 Ervadene Evans Wangler; 1950- 51 Mary Richardson Myas; 1957-58 Clara Spencer

Students:

Adams: Donald **Bartels:** Albert, Freda, Anna **Belknap:** Willie **Belnap:** Eddie, Charlie, Frankie **Blair:** Merrill, Henry, Gerald, Joe, Harry, Josie, Addie, Margaret, Virgil, Edward **Blane:** Harry **Boddy:** Charlie, Robert, Anna **Bohley:** Anna, Bertha, Vernia, Wilbert **Chase:** Veda, Verba, Leonard **Conrad:** Nancy **Dolph:** Bill **Everitt:** Evelyn **Fritz:** Ada; **Gussman:** Paul, Hattie, Walter, Henry **Harris:** Flynt **Kohn:** Cearil, Clarence **Krugh:** Emma, George **Mathews:** Neal **Meadows:** Nellie, Marion, Ralph, Hattie **Moyer:** Donald **Peters:** Viola, Hazel, Herman **Reetz:** Edward, Charles, Clarence, Mabel, Gladys, Helen, Doris Jean, Dwight, George **Remer:** Willie, Ella **Rowland:** Floyd **Schneider:** Ronald, John, Elmer, Gerald, Doris, Ernest, Ervin; **Spencer:** Lelah, Cordia, Nellie **Spierling:** Charlie **Thornton:** Cecil, Iva **Twiliger:** May **Valley:** Ray **Vaughn:** Shirley, Sarah, Amos **Wheeler:** Paul, Pat

EVERGREEN SCHOOL
(Originally named Peters School)

Klacking Township (Town 23 North Range 2 East) NW ¼ of SW ¼ of Section 12 on Campbell Road The original school was built on the Peters farm. The school was moved from the Peters farm in Klacking Twp. to the present site and named evergreen, because it sat beneath evergreen trees.

Alta Goff taught the Peters school 1901-02. Within the next year the school was moved a half mile north on Campbell Road among evergreen trees, and was thereafter called the Evergreen School.

In 1911 the school board consisted of Louis Cumming, Fred W. Reetz, and Charles Antill.

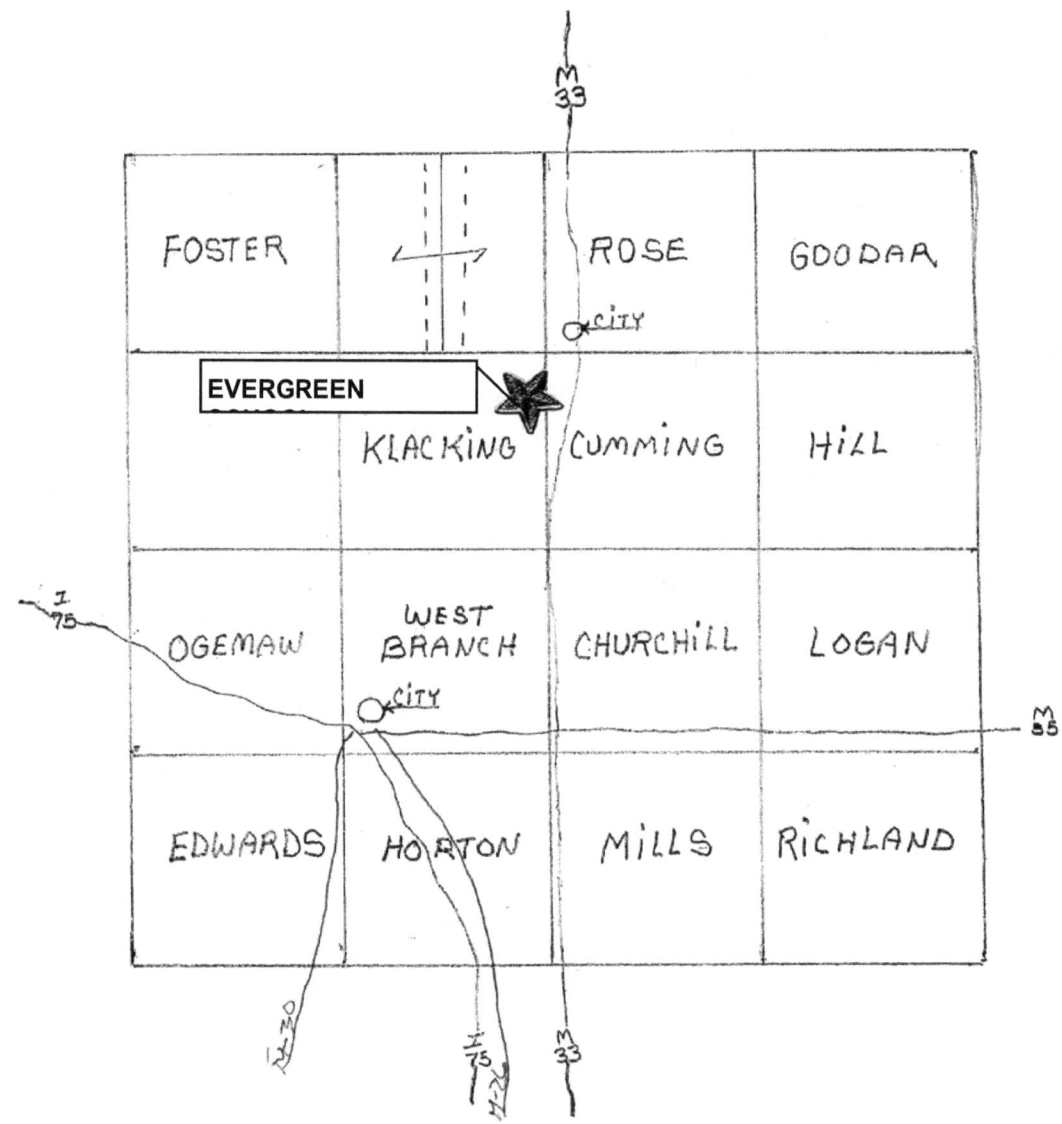

EVERGREEN SCHOOL

(Originally named Peters School)

1901 - 1902

PETERS

PUBLIC SCHOOL.

District No. 2.
Klacking Tp., Ogemaw Co., Mich.
ALTA F. GOFF, Teacher.

1901-1902

PUPILS.

Charlie Spiering	Willie Remer
Ralph Meadows	Charlie Belnap
Eddie Belnap	Cecil Thornton
Albert Bartels	Frankie Belnap
George Krugh	Floyd Rowland
Charlie Boddy	Robert Boddy
Herman Peters	Ella Remer
Cordia Spencer	Nellie Spencer
Bertha Bohley	Emma Krugh
Vernia Boddy	Anna Boddy
Freda Bartels	Iva Thornton
Hattie Meadows	Anna Bartels
Nellie Meadows	Addie Blair
Josie Blair	E. G. May Twiliger

SCHOOL BOARD.

Fred Reetz,	-	Director.
Frank Thornton,	-	Moderator.
Chas. Peters,	-	Assessor.

The Peters School was moved from the NE¼ of NE¼ of Sec. 14 on the Peters farm in Klacking Twp. into Sec. 12. The year is not known. It was then named Evergreen school in 1903 because it was situated among evergreen trees.

July 22, 1994: The school was demolished some years ago, but today a modular home is being erected on that site. The owner is unknown.

EVERGREEN SCHOOL
1903 - 1904

Included in photo:

Olive Janson (teacher), Anna Bohley, Belknap Boy, Belknap Boy, Freda Bartels, Herman Peters, Ralph Meadows, Emma Krugh (Gamber), Cook Boy, Charlie Spierling, Willie Belknap, Hattie Meadows, Josie Blair (Bailer), Nellie Meadows (Bailey), Addie Blair, Anna Bartels (Collins), Cook Girl, Cook Girl

EVERGREEN SCHOOL
1911

Though lost to sight to memory dear
Thou ever will remain;
One only hope my heart can cheer
The hope to meet again.

My Dear Pupil:

THIS BOOKLET SMALL, ARTISTIC, NEAT,
TO YOU A GIFT I MAKE,
AND HOPE FOR YOU 'TWILL BE A TREAT
IN WHICH WE BOTH PARTAKE

AND OFT AS ON ITS LEAVES YOU LOOK,
YOU'LL THINK OF ME, I KNOW,
AND ALL THE CARE AND TIME I TOOK
TO HELP YOU UPWARD GO.

AND WHEN YOUR NAME THEREIN I READ,
I'LL FONDLY THINK OF YOU,
AND WISH SUCCESS MAY BE YOUR MEED
IN ALL YOU STRIVE TO DO.

AND NOW FAREWELL, MY DEAR YOUNG FRIEND,
WE SEPARATE TO DAY;
MAY GOD YOUR FOOTSTEPS WATCH AND TEND,
AND GUIDE YOU IN LIFE'S WAY.

Sincerely,
Your Teacher

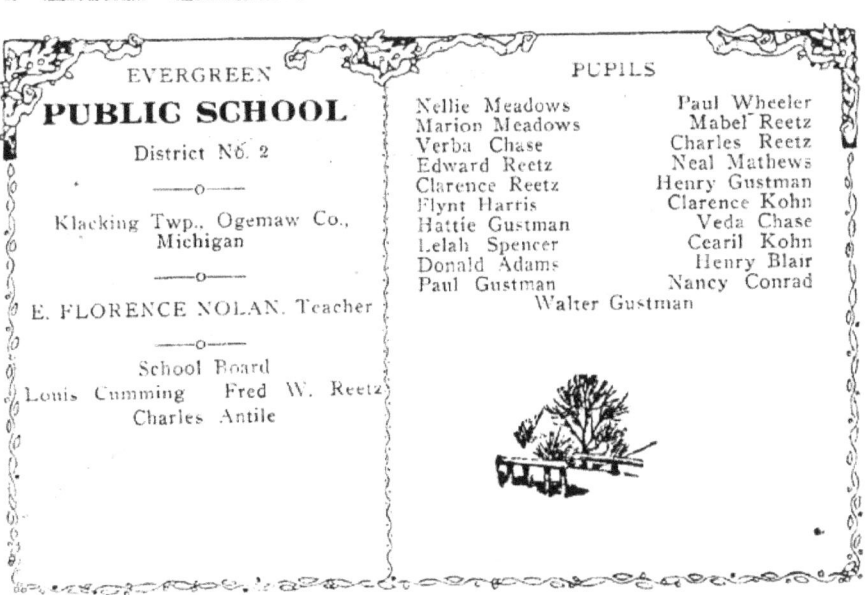

EVERGREEN
PUBLIC SCHOOL
District No. 2

Klacking Twp., Ogemaw Co., Michigan

E. FLORENCE NOLAN, Teacher

School Board
Louis Cumming   Fred W. Reetz
Charles Antile

PUPILS

Nellie Meadows — Paul Wheeler
Marion Meadows — Mabel Reetz
Verba Chase — Charles Reetz
Edward Reetz — Neal Mathews
Clarence Reetz — Henry Gustman
Flynt Harris — Clarence Kohn
Hattie Gustman — Veda Chase
Lelah Spencer — Cearil Kohn
Donald Adams — Henry Blair
Paul Gustman — Nancy Conrad
Walter Gustman

EVERGREEN SCHOOL
1911

Front Row:

Charles Reetz, Cearil Kohn, Walter Gussman, Veda Chase, Verba Chase, Flynt Harris, Edward Reetz, Clarence Reetz

Back Row:

Mabel Reetz, Lelah Spencer, Nancy Conrad, Nellie Meadows, E. Florence Nolan (teacher), Marion Meadows, Hattie Gussman (tallest), Paul Wheeler, Clarence Kohn, Henry Blair, Paul Gussman

EVERGREEN SCHOOL
After 1913

Included in Photo:

Gladys Reetz, Viola Peters, Hazel Peters, Merrill Blair, Verba Chase, Helen Reetz, Charles Reetz, Leonard Chase, Clarence Reetz, two Gussman children, Lottie Meadows (teacher), Veda Chase, Mabel Reetz, Henry Blair, Flynt Harris

EVERGREEN SCHOOL
1930 - 1931

Included in Photo:

Gerald Blair, Bill Dolph, George Reetz, Doris Jean Reetz, Marie E. Buhlman (teacher), Joe Blair, Dwight Reetz, Harry Blair

EVERGREEN SCHOOL

Ogemaw County Herald

April, 1938

EVERGREEN SCHOOL GAINS AWARD FOR XMAS SEAL SALE

School Given Book Set by T. B. Ass'n. Officials

Among Ogemaw county rural schools, top honors for selling 1937 tuberculosis Christmas seals go to children of the Evergreen school, announced the Michigan Tuberculosis Association this week. For winning the highest per capita rating of any other rural school enrollment in Ogemaw county, the children were awarded a set of six Big Books of Adventure Stories —Kidnaped, Robinson Crusoe, Hans Brinker, The Dog of Flanders, Wolf Ear the Indian, and the Dragon's Teeth. The prize was sent them in care of their teacher, Miss Therese Slater, who supervised the sale.

Students at Evergreen school are: Joseph Blair, Ray Valley, Margaret Blair, Elmer Schneider, Wilbert Bohley, Virgil Blair, Donald Moyer, Gerald Schneider, Doris Schneider, Edward Blair, Ernest Schneider and Ervin Schneider.

Second prize, a book of fascinating Indian legends titled "Why the Owl Flies at Night," was won by the pupils at East Side school.

Congratulations of the Michigan Tuberculosis Association were extended to both schools by Theodore J. Werle, executive secretary of the Association. It is a privilege, declared Mr. Werle, to work each year with the rural school children and teachers.

"No small achievement has it been to maintain so fine a record," he pointed out. In doing so, the children and teachers again are helping to safeguard themselves, as well as other Michigan people, from the threat of the White Plague."

Sincerely appreciated is the fine spirit of cooperation and enthusiasm of every school in the Christmas seal sale, Mr. Werle said. Emphasis was placed on the important health work made possible through Christmas seal pennies. Health education and case-finding, Mr. Werle explained are two very important weapons against tuberculosis which Michigan schools help to make possible by selling tuberculosis Christmas seals.

EVERGREEN SCHOOL
1948

Vaughn's, Joan Morgan Green, Teacher

EVERGREEN SCHOOL
1948

Ronald Schneider, Evelyn Everitt, Sarah Vaughn, Shirley Vaughn, John Schneider, and Amos Vaughn? with teacher Joan Morgan Green. Visiting the Court House

EVERGREEN SCHOOL

GENERAL INFORMATION

THE SCHOOLS

In the 1870's and 1880's, when lumber companies plundered Michigan's virgin forest, many families moved north to buy land and establish schools for their children. At first, children were taught to read and write in their homes. As more and more people came, communities sprang up and the men got together and built a schoolhouse.

Many of the first ones were log cabins. They were often one room, one or two windows and one door to the outside. There were usually two outhouses, one for boys and one for girls. Through the years, the buildings got bigger and more numerous.

The country schools offered education to students in Beginners (five years old) through eighth grade of age sixteen. At that time they had a choice of quitting to work or to find transportation to the nearest high school to complete their education -- providing they had passed the eighth grade test.

For over seventy-five years, many of the children growing up in Ogemaw County went to a one room rural school.

THE TEACHERS

At first teachers were hired right out of high school by passing a test. They were usually hired for a three month term. The terms were: January through March, April through June, and September through December. This division of three terms explains why some years have two or three teachers listed for one school. Most of the early teachers were female as the boys often went right to work with their fathers on the farm or in the woods. Donna Valley Nelson got some good advice as she began teaching her first school at age 17. She put a 4-inch piece of rubber hose across her desk -- and had no trouble with her students.

Later, when County Normal was introduced, the women could attend for one year, and then teach while continuing to take classes toward a degree. Many teachers taught the annual school term to earn the money to attend college classes and gain necessary credits to obtain their renewal of certification (and many went on to earn their Bachelor's Degree). It took many years to earn the credits -- summer sessions, Saturday classes, extension classes in the evening and correspondence courses by mail. Usually, when a degree was earned the teacher went to a public school to teach. Teachers then taught the full year and received more pay.

In 1939 one teacher agreed to $65 a month for nine months. There would be nine grades, with Beginners through the eighth grade, and subject areas were reading, penmanship, arithmetic, hygiene, agriculture, grammar, and spelling. They were also expected to teach the evils of smoking and alcohol. Teaching hours were usually 8 a.m. to 4 p.m. They were also expected to tend the heating of the building and the cleaning and care of both the inside of the building and the outside. They must assure that each eighth grade student passed the county examination in order to go to high school. The school director gave a huge envelope of directives from the State School Superintendent's office describing in detail what and how to teach in each subject at each grade level.

Many families took turns boarding the teacher, who received very little pay. In the early years, young women did not teach for long periods of time as they were required to quit their teaching jobs once they married. Alice Thompson was the first married teacher in Ogemaw County.

THE SCHOOL TEACHER'S CREED

I believe in boys and girls, the men and women of tomorrow; that whatsoever the boy soweth, the man shall reap.

I believe in the curse of ignorance, in the efficiency of schools, in the dignity of teaching, and the joy of serving others.

I believe in wisdom as revealed in human lives as well as in the pages of a printed book, in lessons taught, not so much by precept as by example, in ability to work with the hands as well as think with the head -- in everything that makes life large and lovely.

I believe in laughter, in love, in faith, in all ideals and distant hopes that lure us on.

I believe that every hour of every day we receive a just reward for all we are and all we do.

I believe in the present and its opportunities, in the future and its promise and in the divine joy of living.

RULES FOR TEACHERS
1872

1. Teachers each day will fill lamps, clean chimneys.

2. Each teacher will bring a bucket of water and a scuttle of coal for the day's session.

3. Make your pens carefully. You may whittle nibs to the individual taste of the pupils.

4. Men teachers may take one evening each week for courting purposes, or two evenings a week if they go to church regularly.

5. After ten hours in school, the teachers may spend the remaining time reading the Bible or other good books.

6. Women teachers who marry or engage in unseemly conduct will be dismissed.

7. Every teacher should lay aside from each pay a goodly sum of his earning for his benefit during his declining years so that he will not become a burden on society.

8. Any teacher who smokes, uses liquor in any form, frequents pool or public halls, or gets shaved in a barber shop will give good reason to suspect his worth, intention, integrity and honesty.

9. The teacher who performs his labor faithfully and without fail for five years will be given an increase of twenty-five cents per week in his pay, providing the Board of Education approves.

PUNISHMENTS
November, 1893

1. Boys and Girls Playing Together - 4 Lashes
2. Fighting at School - 5 Lashes
3. Quarreling at School - 5 Lashes
4. Gambling or Betting at School - 4 Lashes
5. Playing at Cards at School - 10 Lashes
6. Climbing for Every Foot Over Three Feet Up a Tree - 1 Lash
7. Telling Lies - 7 Lashes
8. Telling Tales Out of School - 8 Lashes
9. Giving Each Other Ill Names - 3 Lashes
10. Swearing at School - 8 Lashes
11. For Misbehaving to Girls - 10 Lashes
12. For Drinking Spirituous Liquors at School - 8 Lashes
13. Making Swings and Swinging on Them - 7 Lashes
14. For Wearing Long Finger Nails - 2 Lashes
15. Misbehaving to Persons on the Road - 4 Lashes
16. For Going to Girls Play Places - 3 Lashes
17. Girls Going to Boys Play Places - 3 Lashes
18. Coming to School with Dirty Faces and Hands - 2 Lashes
19. For Calling Each Other Liars - 4 Lashes
20. For Wrestling at School - 4 Lashes
21. For Wetting Each Other Washing at Playtime - 2 Lashes
22. Scuffling at School - 4 Lashes
23. For Going and Playing about the Mill or Creek - 6 Lashes
24. For Going about the Barn or Doing Any Mischief about the Place - 7 Lashes

COUNTRY SCHOOL REUNIONS

The Ogemaw County Country School Reunion is held the second week in July at the Logan Township Hall. It is pot luck and a good time is had by all.

In 2009, Palmer School had the highest attendance at the Country School Reunion.

In 2010 the Red School had the highest attendance at the Country School Reunion.

BITS AND PIECES

Sherman School was on Campbell Road in the 1880's. Sleighton donated the land.

Two schools have a legal description in Foster Township, but are not named. The descriptions are: SE 1/4 of SW 1/4 of Section 1 and SE 1/4 of SW 1/4 of Section 4.

Miss Cooks was the county music teacher and came around to prepare the children for the spring music festival. The first one was held in May, 1929.

Ernie Thompson did the janitor work for O'Neil School for $45 a month.

County Normal closed in 1945.

Suggestion to parents: In the 1927-1928 school year, parents were asked that if any misunderstandings would arise between pupils and teachers, or between parents and teachers, it would be wise for parents to visit the teacher and calmly and good naturedly yet earnestly talk the matter over. If all concerned used good judgment on such occasions, difficulties could almost always be amicably settled and the school would be the better for it.

OGEMAW COUNTY HERALD

June 9, 1938

Ogemaw County Eighth Grade Graduates

June 9, 1938

Churchill 2—Don Bryan
Churchill 3:
  Robert Barrett
  Gladys Brindley
  Burt Parliament
  Tom Sheppard
  Lawrence Vogan
  Wellesley Vogan
Churchill 3, frl.:
  Agnes Holshoe
  Twila Mason
  Harold Switzer
Cumming 4: Blaine Shattuck
Edwards, No. 1:
  Lucille Bohnard
  Arzell Clayton
  Margery Chapman
  Jack Anderson
  Richard Poplawski
  Dorothy Tuttle
Edwards No. 2:
  Georgia Farmer
  Ernest Gildner
  Jerome Illig
  Eugene Linseman
  Eugene Rau
Edwards, No. 4:
  Marie Archer
  Don Bowsher
  Eugene McGlashen
  Wilbur Osborne
  Merwin Roach
South Branch:
  Evelyn Hicks
  Lillie Roe
Goodar:
  Catherine Eno
  David Humphrey
  Irwin Lepper
  Betty Senyko
Hill, No. 1:
  Lloyd Bindscheattle
  Virginia Barber
Hill, No. 4:
  Alba Drenberg
Hill, No. 5:
  Olive Thompson
  Valvae Thompson
Horton, 1 frl.:
  Katherine Allen
  Marian Allen
  Wilford Allen
  Junior Hall
Horton, No. 2:
  Barbara Kauffman
  Bernard Scheele
  John Gehl
Horton, No. 3:
  Jack Ehinger
  Irvadene Evans
Klacking No. 1:
  Keith Finerty
Klacking No. 2:
  Joseph Blair
  Ray Valley
Klacking, No. 3:
  Jerald Brick

Harold Brick
Iona Houston
Harry Fritz
Dick Klacking
Ione Meir
Robert Barrett
Logan, No. 1:
  Janice Brindley
Logan, No. 2 frl.
  Lila Adams
  Frank Bennett
  Howard Schult
Logan, No. 4:
  Jack Brown
  Syble Lawrence
Logan, No. 5:
  Louis Best
  Calvin Caverly
  Lillian Clemens
Mills, No. 2:
  Eunice May
  Grace Goatbe
Ogemaw, No. 2:
  Frederick Stehle
Ogemaw, No. 3:
  Buddy Cowles
  Frank Crawford
  Helen Hazeltine
Richland, No. 1:
  Nona Bergquist
  Joyce Bergquist
  Ruth Harmon
  Frances Rye
  Marie Wager
Richland, No. 2:
  William Farro
  Geraldine Steele
Richland, No. 3:
  Irene Finger
  Erma Redfield
  Gorden Redfield
  Alice Remilong
  Doris Thorn
Richland, No. 5 frl.:
  Thelma Hall
Rose No. 3:
  Thelma Barber
  J. R. Teeples
Rose No. 4: Ralph Craddock
West Branch, No. 2:
  Esther Shore
West Branch No. 3:
  Brayton Fisher
  Florence Hacht
  Della Little
  Leo Neubecker
  Forrest Stephens
  Maxine Wangler
West Branch No. 4:
  Melvin LeDuc
  Harriet Osborne
  Lorene Simonis

West Branch No. 5:
  Evan Crow, Jr.
  Annabelle Perkins
  Dorothy Perkins

EIGHTH GRADE EXAMINATION

The Seventh and Eighth grade students in the Rural schools of Michigan had to write State Examinations in May in order to be promoted.

The County Commissioner of Schools and two Examiners conducted the Examinations in West Branch, Rose City, and Prescott.

These Examinations were held annually from the early days until 1934.

When the County Commissioner of Schools was not satisfied with the ratings of our students, she stressed the need for the teachers to work with the 7th and 8th students to review and concentrate on the subjects for the State Examinations.

The 8th grade students in the country schools had to pass an exam in May in order to be promoted. The County Commissioner of Schools and two examiners conducted the exam. They were held annually from the early days until 1934. If the County commissioner was not satisfied with the ratings of the students, the teachers had to work with the students ahead of the exam, and concentrate on the subjects being tested.

EIGHTH GRADE EXAMINATION

Questions prepared by the Superintendent of Public Instruction for the regular examination, May 13-14, 1920.

AGRICULTURE

Answer any ten.

1. Give three reasons why agriculture should be taught.
2. (a) Explain what is meant by surface soil, (b) subsoil.
3. Name four kinds of plants that are raised primarily for their leaves and stalks.
4. Is it a good practice to rake leaves into the road and burn them? Give reason for your answer.
5. Would you consider manure or commercial fertilizers the better form of fertilizer for sandy soil? Why?
6. What system of crop rotation do the farmers in your community use? Do you consider it a good rotation? Give your reasons.
7. Name the cereals commonly raised in your community. What are their uses?
8. (a) Why are potatoes such a popular and important article of diet? (b) Name the common variety of potatoes grown in your community. (c) Which one do you prefer? (d) Why?
9. Name five injurious insects in your community. How do you eradicate each?
10. What breeds of poultry are common in your community? Which breed do you prefer? Why?
11. Name the common breeds of swine in your community. Which breed do you prefer? Why?
12. Describe how some good roads have been built in your county.

ARITHMETIC

60 Credits

1. Draw a plan showing the sections of a township. Locate sections 9 and 22.
2. A Boy Scout sold 75 Liberty Loan Bonds of the $50 denomination and 14 of the $100 denomination. What was the total amount of these sales?
3. How many years, months, and days will elapse before you will be 21 years old?
4. At 24 cents a square foot what will it cost to lay a 6 foot concrete walk on two sides of a corner lot 50×100 feet?
5. Make out a bill of the following goods bought by John Jones of Loftus' Grocery Company: 34 cans peas at 11c; 50 cans corn at 12½c; and 60 cans tomatoes at 16c. Receipt the bill.
6. Find the interest on $250 for 3 yrs. 5 mo. 12 da., at 6%.

MENTAL ARITHMETIC

40 Credits

Note: Examiners distribute problems face down. At a signal applicants turn papers over and using pencils for writing answers only, solve as many as possible in 30 minutes.

	Answer
1. What bills and coins are required to pay a man $3.65?	1.
2. Out of an income of $1200 a family saves each year 12%. How much does this amount to a month?	2.
3. How many feet of lumber in a piece of timber 1 in. thick, 1 ft. wide and 8 ft. long?	3.
4. What will it cost to insure a house for $5,000 at $.20 a hundred?	4.
5. A baseball team won 16 games, which was 2/3 of the number of games played. How many games did they play?	5.
6. If a man rents a house for $400 a year, how much is this per month?	6.
7. Write in figures: two hundred one ten thousandths.	7.
8. A dealer sells a coat marked $120 at a discount of 33⅓%. How much does he receive for the coat?	8.
9. If 2 acres of land yield 300 bushels of potatoes, how many bushels of potatoes should 3 such acres produce?	9.
10. How many gallons of molasses will be needed to fill 272 tin cans, each containing 1 pint?	10.
11. Change to a common fraction 40%, 66⅔%.	11.
12. Change to an equivalent per cent ¾, ⅞.	12.
13. What is the interest on $50 for 2 yr. 6 mo. at 5%?	13.
14. How many square inches in ½ square foot?	14.
15. A boy finds that the distance around his father's automobile wheel is 10 ft. How many times does the wheel turn around in going over the distance of 1 mile?	15.
16. How much picture molding will it take to go around a room 30 ft. long and 20 ft. wide?	16.
17. A cellar is 36 ft. long, 18 ft. wide and 6 ft. deep. How many cubic yards of dirt were removed in digging it?	17.
18. Give all the numbers that are perfect squares from 1 to 25.	18.
19. Find the cost of 5 bushels of potatoes at $2.50.	19.
20. Find the cost of 100 lbs. meal at $.02½.	20.
21. Find the cost of one map when 24 maps cost $192.	21.
22. In how many weeks can a boy save enough to buy a Liberty Bond costing $100, if he saves $2.50 each week?	22.
23. Change 39 inches to feet and inches.	23.
24. How many quarts in 25 gallons?	24.
25. Write in Roman numerals: 52, 119, 120	25.
26. Multiply 30.61 by 10.	26.
27. Reduce to lowest terms: 22/24, 16/18.	27.
28. What is the Greatest Common Divisor of 18 and 42?	28.
29. A rug is 8½ ft. wide. At $.50 a foot, find the cost of a fringe for both ends of the rug.	29.
30. A Boy Scout's record for walking was 9¾ miles, but he increased this record to 12⅝ miles. How many miles did he increase his record?	30.

31. $1/4 + 3/8 + 5/16 =$

32. $8/15 \div 3 =$

33. $.008 \overline{)2.56}$

34. $72 \div 8/9 =$

35.	36.	37.	38.
$9/10 \div 3/5 =$	$\dfrac{12 \times 56}{7 \times 16} =$	$1800 \times .33\tfrac{1}{3}$	$\$5.00 - 3.18$

39.	40.
lb oz 10 11 +10 9	$275\tfrac{5}{8}$ $-49\tfrac{1}{4}$

CIVIL GOVERNMENT.

1. What is the difference between a pure democracy and a republic? Which form of government have we in this country?
2. What is meant by the term citizen?
3. Tell three things that a government should do for its citizens.
4. State two things that every citizen owes his government.
5. What township officers are elected annually?
6. What qualifications must persons have to vote in Michigan?
7. Why is it the duty of every legal voter to vote in all township, county, and state elections?
8. What are the duties of a township supervisor?
9. How does a good prosecuting attorney in your county benefit the people of your township?
10. What is the chief executive officer of a township, a county, a state, the nation?

GEOGRAPHY

1. (a) Explain the climate of Washington and Oregon.
   (b) Compare this climate with that of the states just east of them.
2. What and where are the following? Serbia, Panama, Yosemite, Bengal, Borneo, Sahara, Capricorn, Gulf Stream, Gibraltar, Metz, Himalaya. (Answer any eight.)
3. Explain fully the condensation of moisture on the window pane of your mother's kitchen. How does this observation help you to understand and explain a fall of rain or snow?
4. Mention five things which would enter into the choice of a location for a large manufacturing plant.
5. Michigan has a combination of physical features such as no other state possesses. Tell how these have been a benefit and how they have determined the life and industries of the people.
6. How would you go by water from Petrograd to Constantinople?
7. Locate two world centers of each of the following products: wheat, coal, iron, cotton, coffee.
8. State something important concerning five Michigan cities.
9. Give three good examples of each of the following sorts of vegetation regions, and state briefly the cause for such vegetation: tundras, deserts, jungles, open forests, grassy plains.
10. Name six river systems of North America and tell which you consider of the greatest importance. Give your reasons.

GRAMMAR

1. Write the plural of these words: calf, piano, sheep, lily, handful, Miss, loaf, enemy, turkey.
2. Name the eight parts of speech. Define any four.
3. Write a simple sentence, a complex sentence, and a compound sentence.
4. Tell how the nouns in these sentences are used:
   The brook trickles down the hill.
   He brought the flower to his favorite teacher, Miss Brown.
5. Write three rules for the use of capital letters. Illustrate each.

6. Correct these sentences:
   John throwed the ball to Jim.
   I could of gone yesterday.
   Where is the book at?
   I don't see no buds.
   He laid on the couch all day.
7. Write two sentences. Underline the complete subject of each sentence once. Underline the complete predicates twice.
8. Write a sentence containing:
   (a) a prepositional phrase
   (b) a clause
   (c) a possessive noun
9. Select the complements in these sentences and tell what kind they are:
   A rolling stone gathers no moss.
   Some plants are poisonous.
   Her voice was ever soft.
   Fear made the soldiers pale.
10. Fill the blanks with the correct word:
    You and――――(me, I) will go together.
    Every girl may keep what――――(she, they)――――(has, have) earned.
    Come into the house and――――(sit, set) down.
    Our dog likes to――――(lay, lie) in the sun.

ORTHOGRAPHY

1. Use the following words in sentences so as to show the difference in meaning:

root	route
serge	surge
berth	birth
cellar	seller
knead	need

2. Give the meanings of the following prefixes and illustrate each with a word: circum, semi, pro, tri, re, uni, anti, dis, auto, sub.
3. Mark the vowels in the following words: small, gold, king, spade, look, song, drag, wheat, lark, dirt.
4. Add *ing* to the following: come, oblige, see, swim, forget, hoe.
5. Name three different kinds of information that can be found in the dictionary.

SPELLING

To the Examiner: In marking papers, orthography should count fifty per cent and spelling fifty per cent.

1. many
2. pretty
3. ninety
4. straight
5. Tuesday
6. hoarse
7. ready
8. writing
9. buy
10. wedding
11. breeze
12. except
13. president
14. choose
15. railroad
16. unable
17. expense
18. making
19. courage
20. guest
21. mariner
22. pilot
23. objection
24. together
25. busy
27. serious
26. business
28. absence
29. senate
30. heard

(Dictate the following for the pupils to write. The spelling of the words in italics should count in the examination. Read without designating the words on which the spelling is to be based).

It is *rather* for us to be *here dedicated* to the great task *remaining* before us,— that from these *honored* dead we take *increased devotion* to that *cause* for *which* they gave the last full *measure* of devotion; that we here *highly resolve* that these dead shall not have *died* in *vain*; that this *nation* under God, shall have a new *birth* of *freedom;* and that *government* of the *people*, by the people, and for the people shall not *perish* from the *earth*.—Lincoln's Gettysburg Address.

PENMANSHIP

1. Write the capital letters of the alphabet.
2. Write five times on separate lines: Michigan became a State January 26, 1837.
3. Write the first stanza of *America*. The first stanza of *The Star Spangled Banner*.

PHYSIOLOGY

1. (a) What habits of health should be practiced by every boy and girl of your age?
   (b) What reasons can you give for trying to have a healthy body?
2. (a) Why should a room occupied by many people be well ventilated?
   (b) Why should one sleep with his window wide open?
3. What would you do before a doctor came if you were alone with someone who was suffering from one of the following: frozen feet or fingers, a bad cut which bled seriously, sprained ankle or wrist, fainting. (Write of one only).
4. Give five frequent causes of poor eyesight and suggest a remedy for each.
5. Why is it necessary to keep the body clean if one wishes to be healthy? How frequently is it necessary to take a full warm bath? What may be done to avoid taking cold after a bath?
6. (a) Give three good reasons for standing and sitting straight.
   (b) How is the blood purified when you play hard out of doors?
   (c) Why is it necessary to be very careful about the elimination of waste from the body?
7. What is the relation of good food and good digestion to good health?
8. What are the food elements necessary for the life and growth of the body? Name a food that is rich in each of these.
9. Name some common diseases which are easily spread from one individual to another. What can you do to prevent the spread of such diseases?
10. Write what you know about one of the following: digestion of the food, circulation of the blood, how the blood overcomes disease, the nature and care of the teeth.

READING

1. The Rime of the Ancient Mariner is the tale of strange things that happened to a mariner and his crew.
   (a) What was the cause of their bad luck on this trip?
   (b) What is an albatross?
2. Who is the person that tells this strange story? To whom is he talking?
3. Why do you think the Wedding Guest stayed to hear the story instead of going to the wedding as he had intended?
4. Why did the Mariner kill the Albatross?
5. Mention some of the disasters that came to the Mariner and his crew after the Albatross had been killed.
6. What is a *phantom ship?*

7. Just when did the Mariner begin to feel like blessing all living creatures? What happened immediately?
8. Prove by some incidents in the poem that the physical appearance of the Ancient Mariner was greatly changed when he returned.
9. Write from memory two stanzas of the poem.
10. Tell briefly how the poem came to be written.

U. S. HISTORY

1. What is Armistice Day? Why do we celebrate it?
2. What nations settled in the territory occupied by the thirteen colonies? What nation finally ruled them?
3. Why was a new constitution adopted in 1789?
4. How and why did we get the Philippine Islands;
5. Tell something of each of the following men: General Grant, Lafayette, Admiral Dewey, Admiral Sims, General Pershing, General Foch, John Adams, Andrew Jackson.
6. Name some inventions which have made farm work much easier.
7. How were the states of the Mississippi valley settled, and why?
8. What was the Louisiana Purchase? What were the results?
9. How did we get our soldiers and sailors for the war with Germany?
10. What do you understand by, (a) the tariff; (b) government ownership of railroads; (c) our trouble with Mexico; (d) free silver; (e) Federal Reserve Bank.

MICHIGAN EDUCATIONAL STATISTICS
A FIFTY YEAR COMPARISON

Student Enrollment by Grades in Michigan Public Schools
at Close of Year, (1920)
And on the Fourth Friday Following Labor Day: (1970)

Grade	1920	1970
K	59,148	169,329
1	97,999	169,462
2	71,433	167,056
3	68,151	164,207
4	68,438	166,628
5	65,594	163,550
6	61,893	162,530
7	55,287	169,384
8	50,448	166,416
9	23,412	170,736
10	14,255	165,094
11	11,987	147,911
12	9,658	129,051
Other	—	67,392
Total	657,701	2,178,746

	1920	1970
School population	978,412	2,775,707 a
Public school enrollment	663,948	2,178,746
Number of ungraded school districts	6,580	—
Number of graded school districts	693	638 b
Total	7,273	
Number of township school districts	169	—
Number of school houses	8,922	— c
Estimated value of school property	$102,626,507	—
Average school year in months	8.8	9.5
Total number of teachers employed	24,302	87,499
Total wages of teachers	$23,891,537	$965,463,966
Average wages of teachers per month -		
Males	$156.51 (14.1%)d	$1,180 (34.5%)
Females	$102.81 (85.9%)	$1,100 (65.5%)
Average annual wage of teachers	$983.10	$11,034 e
Average student teacher ratio	27.3	24.9
Average annual per pupil expenditures	$76.63	$821.63
School completion Ratio -		
H.S. or More	(Est.) 10% 34.9%	52.8%
8th Gr. or More	(Est.) 60% (1950)	Persons 25 yrs. or older

(a) Age 5-19 yrs.
(b) 530 H.S. Dist.; 96 Non H.S. Dist.; 12 Non Operating Dist.
(c) Public Schools 1971-72; 2503 Elem.; 1359 Sec.; 43 Comb.
(d) National Percentages of Male & Female Teachers
(e) **Average Annual**

Money Earnings U.S.A.	1920		1970
Public Education Teacher	$970		$8,141
Federal Govt. Employee	$1,707		$10,597
Contract Construction Worker	$2,620		$10,140
All Workers	$1,342		$7,564
Mich. Per Capita Income	—	$794 (1929)	$4,156
U.S. Per Capita Income	$562		$3,966
Median Family Income	—		$9,867

Sample Food Costs

	1920	1970
Bread	.11¢ lb.	.24¢ lb.
Round Steak	.39¢ lb.	1.30¢ lb.
Chuck Roast	.26¢ lb.	.72¢ lb.
Flour 5 lb.	.40¢	.59¢
Milk 1/2 gal.	.33¢	.57¢
Consumer Price Index 1967 = 100	60.0 CPI	116.3 CPI

Auto Costs

	1920	1970
6 cyl. Oldsmobile	$1,535	$2,664

The Country Schools of Ogemaw County: Volume 1

TEACHER INDEX

Abbott, Ansel (Atherton)
Addison, Linis (Damon)
Aikins, Fred (Damon)
Alenger, Marie (Erb)
Andrews, Florence (Eastside, Edwards)
Angerer, John (Edwards)
Artman, Helen (Edwards)
Atherton, Gertrude (Busenbark, Bush Lake, Deckerville)
Babcock, M. (Cook)
Ballantine, Thomas (Eastside)
Barnham (Atherton)
Belson, Beatrice (Cook)
Bemis, Velma Crawford (Deckerville)
Bennett, Florence Freed (Campbell Corners)
Bennett, Madaline (Busenbark)
Bennett, Mrs. (Damon)
Bishop, Florence (Cook, Edwards)
Bixby, Eleanore (Evergreen)
Black, Linda (Eastside)
Black, Mrs. (Cranberry Lake)
Blackledge, Lorene (Dale)
Blakley, DeWayne (Damon)
Blakley, Mattie (Dale, Damon)
Boddy, Dora (Atherton)
Brick, Thelma Reetz (Erb)
Brown, Miss (Eastside)
Brunges, Hazel (Bush Lake)
Buckel, Elizabeth (Erb)
Buckel, Marie (Erb)
Buckingham, Ada (Eastside)
Buckingham, Vynne (Eastside)
Buhlman, Beverly (Erb)
Buhlman, Marie (Cook, Edwards, Erb, Evergreen)
Bullock, Fred (Campbell Corners)
Burgess, Mary Smith (Beechwood)
Butler, Francis Nelson (Eastside)
Campbell, Elizabeth Pillsbury (Campbell Corners)
Carpenter, Ethlyn (Cranberry Lake)
Carr, Gertrude (Eastside)
Carscallen, Hildreth Webster (Campbell Corners)
Cascadden, Leona Holt (Erb)
Chambers, Ruth (Deckerville)
Chase, Verba (Evergreen)
Church, Helen Decker (Cook)
Clark, Dennis (Atherton)
Clark, Virginia Simmons (Atherton, Eastside)
Combs, Nellie (Erb)
Cook, Jennie (Bell)
Cooley, Clarence (Atherton)
Crawford, Wilma Oliver (Campbell Corners)
Cripps, Lolita (Erb)
Crow, Edith (Caverly)
Cummings, Orville (Eastside)
Dankin, Fred W. (Damon)
David, Helen (Atherton, Bush Lake)
Decker, Dorothy (Campbell Corners, Cook)
Decker, Helen (Eastside)
DeMatio, Donald (Atherton)
DeMatio, Joseph (Beechwood)
DeMatio, Robert (Edwards)

Ogemaw County Genealogical & Historical Society

TEACHER INDEX Continued

Dennis, Francis M. (Cook)

Dennis, Rosella (Bell, Dale, Eastside)

Dennis, Rosella Polmanteer (Atherton, Bell)

Derenick, Eleanor (Atherton)

Dikos, Mary (Cook)

Dodds, Harrison (Atherton)

Dodds, Minnie Bennett (Atherton)

Dunlap, A. L. (Dale)

Eckelson, Ethel (Busenbark)

Ehinger, Marie (Erb)

Embury, Maud (Bell)

Engel, Ethel (Bush Lake)

Evans, Helen (Campbell Corners)

Fegan, Bernard (Busenbark, Bush Lake, Cranberry Lake)

Flint, Muriel (Edwards)

Ford, J. E. (Cook)

Foster, Edward (Edwards)

Franklin, Coral (Dale)

Freeman, Harold (Dale)

Fritz, Ada (Dale, Eastside)

Fuhrman, William (Beechwood, Campbell Corners)

Furman, Mary Edwards (Deckerville)

Gates, Bertha (Damon)

Gillam, Myrta (Eastside)

Goff, Alta (Evergreen)

Goff, Mina (Cook)

Goodrich, Bernetta Finerty (Bell)

Graber, Bertina DeKett (Beechwood)

Grawburg, Arlene (Evergreen)

Gray, Marion (Busenbark)

Green, Joan (Cook, Evergreen)

Green, Marion (Damon, Eastside)

Gregg, Howard (Cranberry Lake)

Hacht, Alma (Campbell Corners)

Hall, Vera Parliament (Dale)

Hammond, Mary (Dale)

Harcourt, Theresa (Beechwood)

Harris, E. M. (Eastside)

Harrison, Jennie (Cranberry Lake)

Hart, Edra (Damon)

Hartsell, Mary (Busenbark)

Hayes, Mrs. (Erb)

Heath, Anna Walker (Atherton, Bell)

Hewitt, Margaret Beemer (Edwards)

Holshoe, Ivadelle (Campbell Corners)

Holt, Florence (Edwards)

Hooper, Lucille Kennedy (Cook)

Howard, Rachel McKellar (Dale)

Howe, Margaret Freeborn (Atherton)

Humphrey, Mac (Campbell Corners)

Hustee, Amy Richardson (Edwards)

Husted, Emma (Eastside)

Husted, Margaret (Cook, East Side)

Ide, Gladys (Beechwood)

Illig, Anna Mae (Cook, Eastside, Edwards, Erb)

Janson, Olive (Evergreen)

Jardine, Mr. (Busenbark)

Jenson, Cora E. (Dale)

Jones, Lavina (Atherton)

Jones, Lottie (Campbell Corners)

Kennedy, Hiram (Damon)

Kennedy, Margaret Montell (Eastside)

Kennedy, Pearl E. (Damon)

TEACHER INDEX Continued

Kenyon, Harry (Atherton, Bell)

Kenyon, Marian (Bell)

Kenyon, Maud (Bell)

Kenyon, Mrs. (Bell)

Kleehammer, Ruth (Edwards)

Krengielski, Veronica (Cook, Erb)

Kube, Julianna Reiter (Erb, Evergreen)

Kuhn, Miss (Beechwood, Bell)

LaDue, Mae (Bell)

Lehman, Inez (Cook, Deckerville)

Lince, Louise (Deckerville)

Lince, Myrtle (Deckerville)

Link, Ada Johnson (Edwards)

Loney, Mary Loop (Edwards, Erb, Evergreen)

Lovell, Alice (Campbell Corners)

Madison, Eva Nelson (Cook)

Markell, Lanora (Bell)

Martin, Merle (Cranberry Lake)

Martin, Virginia (Beechwood)

Marx, Gertrude Butler (Beechwood)

Mason, Pearl Rose (Campbell Corners, Evergreen)

Mattel, Margaret (Bush Lake, Campbell Corners)

Matthews, Merle (Bush Lake)

Mattox, Marjory (Erb)

Mayhew, Ethel (Beechwood, Bell)

McCallum, George (Damon)

McCauley, Maggie (Edwards)

McCoy, Irene Miller (Bell, Campbell Corners)

McDonald, Eugenie Rice (Atherton)

McLaren, Kate (Erb)

McLees, Anna (Evergreen)

McLeod, Phoebe Regan (Campbell Corners)

Meadows, Lottie Chambers (Evergreen)

Meddler, Mrs. (Bush Lake)

Merrill, F. A. (Eastside)

Merrill, Mamie (Eastside)

Mier, Irma (Beechwood)

Migan, Helen David (Beechwood, Bell)

Miller, Mary (Damon)

Mills, Mona (Atherton)

Mockridge, Minnie (Damon)

Morris, Loretta (Cook)

Morrison, Mrs. J. W. (Eastside)

Moyer, Leona (Evergreen)

Myas, Mary Richardson (Busenbark, Eastside, Evergreen)

Nelson, Donna Valley (Eastside)

Nelson, Eva (Cook, Eastside)

Nelson, Irene (Eastside)

Nelson, Norma (Eastside)

Netzlaff, Wenona Gibson (Atherton, Campbell Corners)

Nieman, Gertrude Carr (Busenbark)

Nolan, Florence (Evergreen)

Norris, Ada Quigley (Atherton)

Norris, Alla (Campbell Corners)

Norris, Jennie (Eastside)

Nye, Donna (Dale)

Ohl, Alice Klann (Erb)

Paddison, Lizzie (Damon)

Papp, Edward (Deckerville)

Parkinson, Edwina (Eastside)

Pekrul, Muriel Hallgren (Cook)

Perkins, Ida Olsen (Busenbark)

Pickens, Berniece (Bush Lake)

Pillsbury, Pearl (Cranberry Lake)

TEACHER INDEX Continued

Plancher, Grace (Beaver Lake)

Powell, Helen (Erb)

Priest, Cleo (Bush Lake)

Quackenbush, Gladys (Cook)

Quigley, Wilma Gage (Atherton)

Rabidue, Alice (Evergreen)

Rakestraw, Lorene (Atherton)

Rakestraw, Neva Dobson (Damon)

Ranney, George (Beechwood)

Rau, Doris (Cook, Erb)

Rau, Esther Bragg (Cook)

Rau, Evelyn Schneider (Edwards)

Rau, Flora Scheele (Bell)

Raymoure, Lena (Deckerville)

Redman, Mr. (Edwards)

Reetz, Loretta (Campbell Corners)

Reetz, Vera Winter (Cook)

Reid, Beryl (Deckerville)

Reiter, Pauline (Cook)

Rhinehart, Margaret (Busenbark)

Rice, Gladys Reetz (Evergreen)

Richardson, Cora Newberry (Busenbark, Eastside)

Richardson, Georgina (Edwards)

Richardson, Susie (Atherton, Eastside)

Rivers, Joanna (Erb)

Robinson, Betty Candy (Eastside, Edwards)

Rose, Hiram (Evergreen)

Ross, Jenette Swift (Campbell Corners)

Rusher, Cordie (Evergreen)

Rusher, Edith (Bush Lake)

Sarros, Geneva Flynn (Dale)

Scheele, Edward (Campbell Corners, Eastside, Edwards)

Scheele, Flora (Damon)

Schick, Viola (Busenbark, Evergreen)

Sheldon, Olive Pillsbury (Cranberry Lake)

Shepherd, Jessie (Edwards)

Shiel, Edwin (Eastside, Erb, Edwards)

Shrigley, Vera (Edwards)

Slater, Theresa Harcourt (Beechwood, Evergreen)

Smith, Mrs. (Eastside)

Snyder, Harriet (Damon)

Snyder, Marion (Eastside)

Spencer, Clara (Evergreen)

Sturtevant, Helen (Atherton)

Sutton, Cameron (Bell, Erb)

Switzer, Grace Dodds (Atherton, Bell)

Tesch, Olith (Edwards)

Thomas, Blanche Rau (Eastside)

Thompson, Alice Selesky (Campbell Corners)

Thompson, Ethel (Deckerville)

Thompson, Floy (Bell)

Trainor, Belle Bixby (Evergreen)

Turner, Florine (Atherton)

Walker, Emma (Dale)

Walker, Rose (Bush Lake)

Walter, Stanley (Erb)

Wangler, Ervadean Evans (Campbell Corners, Evergreen)

Wangler, Maxine Barber (Campbell Corners, Cook)

Warren, Fanny (Eastside)

Whiteside, Bessie (Deckerville)

Wilcox, Elizabeth (Cook, Erb)

Wilkinson, Ruth Shimmons (Cranberry Lake)

Williams, Alice (Edwards)

Williams, Arzell Walker (Atherton, Campbell Corners)

TEACHER INDEX Continued

Williams, Leota (Edwards)

Winegar, Electa Withey (Atherton, Bell)

Winter, Vera (Campbell Corners)

Witherspoon, Kathleen Williams (Edwards)

Wood, Effie G. (Eastside)

Woodiwiss, Cleo (Cook)

Wright, Joan (Erb)

Yantz, Olive (Erb)

FAMILY NAME INDEX

Adams
 Alice (Campbell Corners)
 Donald (Evergreen)
 George (Campbell Corners)
 Vina (Campbell Corners)

Adkins
 Ruth (Dale)

Adolph
 Albert (Erb)
 Elmer (Erb)

Allen
 Myrtle (Atherton)
 Janet (Eastside)
 Jim (Eastside)
 Judy (Eastside)
 Ralph (Atherton)

Alonzo
 Margie (Cranberry Lake)

Alpin
 Bernice (Edwards)
 Deverne (Edwards)
 Don (Edwards)
 Gilmore (Edwards)
 Vivian (Edwards)

Alvord
 Richard (Dale)

Ammond
 Alice (Campbell Corners)
 Bert (Campbell Corners)
 Clyde (Campbell Corners)
 Etta (Campbell Corners)
 Lizzie (Campbell Corners)
 Ora (Campbell Corners)
 Roy (Campbell Corners)

Anderson
 Bessie (Edwards)
 Clara (Edwards)
 Grace (Edwards)
 Helen (Edwards)
 Jack (Deckerville, Edwards)
 James (Edwards)
 Lucile (Edwards)
 Marilyn (Deckerville)
 Michael (Edwards)
 Robert (Edwards)

Andrews
 Bessie (Edwards)
 Florence (Edwards)
 Harriett (Edwards)
 Leo (Edwards)
 Nancy (Eastside)
 Orrissi (Edwards)
 Sally (Eastside)
 Stanley (Edwards)

Andrus
 Nelson (Campbell Corners)
 Vera (Campbell Corners)

Arntz
 Johnny (Dale)
 Ruben (Dale)

Arthur
 Frankie (Dale)
 Gerald (Dale)

Atherton
 Durfee (Dale)
 Georgia (Dale)
 Johnie (Dale)
 Lillie (Dale)
 Mary (Dale)
 Olivia (Dale)
 Oren (Atherton)
 Rosie (Dale)
 Stella (Dale)
 Susie (Dale)
 Thelda (Atherton)
 Willard (Atherton)
 William (Dale)

Bagley
 Alice (Campbell Corners)
 Beth (Campbell Corners)
 Henry (Campbell Corners)

Bailey
 Georgie (Dale)
 Josephine (Erb)
 Maxine (Erb)

Baldwin
 Ruth (Atherton)

Ballard
 Maude (Busenbark)

Barber
 Bob (Cook)
 Delma (Eastside)
 Elsworth (Eastside)
 Jack (Beechwood)
 Mervin (Beechwood)
 Thelma (Eastside)

Barcia
 LeRoy (Edwards)
 Margy (Edwards)
 Tom (Edwards)

Barley
 Alpha (Edwards)

Barnum
 Harold (Atherton)
 John (Atherton)
 Mildred (Atherton)
 Robert (Atherton)
 Stella (Atherton)

Barringer
 Charlotte (Edwards)
 Clifford (Edwards, Erb)
 Kenneth (Edwards, Erb)
 Lucile (Edwards)

Bartels
 Albert (Evergreen)
 Anna (Evergreen)
 Freda (Evergreen)

Bauman
 Harold (Atherton)

Baumchen
 Frank (Campbell Corners)
 Helena (Campbell Corners)

Beach
 Alex (Campbell Corners)
 Cora (Campbell Corners)
 Della (Campbell Corners)

Beals
 Rosemary (Eastside)

FAMILY NAME INDEX Continued

Beard
W. (Damon)

Beck
Don (Eastside)
Richard (Eastside)

Becker
Florence (Damon)
Fred (Atherton)

Beckwith
May (Edwards)

Bedtelyon
Dean (Campbell Corners)
Don (Campbell Corners)
Luke (Campbell Corners)
Matt (Campbell Corners)

Beemer
Marguerite (Edwards)

Belanger
Arthur (Atherton)
Corrine (Atherton)
Delamae (Atherton)
Emelda (Atherton)
Jack (Atherton)
Louise (Atherton)
Velma (Atherton)

Belknap
Willie (Evergreen)

Bell
Charles (Damon)
Clyde (Damon)
Daisy (Damon)
Ella (Damon)
Kenneth (Erb)

Belnap
Charlie (Evergreen)
Frankie (Evergreen)
Willie (Evergreen)

Bender
Lloyd (Cook)

Benjamin
Beverly (Eastside)
Carol (Eastside)
Gary (Eastside)
Ronald (Eastside)

Bennett
Alberta (Campbell Corners)
Alvin (Campbell Corners)
Betty (Eastside)
Bill (Caverly)
Bob (Caverly)
Butch (Edwards)
Clara (Campbell Corners)
Florence (Campbell Corners)
Frank (Campbell Corners)
Gale (Campbell Corners)
Geraldine (Cook, Edwards)
JoAnn (Campbell Corners)
Gerry (Edwards)
Gladys (Campbell Corners)
Harold (Campbell Corners)
Harvey (Campbell Corners)
Hazel (Campbell Corners)
John (Cook, Edwards)
Johnnie (Campbell Corners)
Judy (Edwards)
Kenneth (Edwards)
Laura (Campbell Corners)
Leo (Cook, Edwards)
LeRoy (Edwards)
Maggie (Campbell Corners)
Mary (Campbell Corners)
Minnie (Campbell Corners)
Ruth (Campbell Corners)
Sam (Campbell Corners)

Bentley
John (Cranberry Lake)
Margaret (Cranberry Lake)
Sarah (Cranberry Lake)
Vera (Eastside)
Vinton (Eastside)
Vivian (Eastside)

Bernor
Alfred (Edwards)
Ruth (Edwards)

Best
Charles (Cranberry Lake)
Clifford (Caverly)
Fannie (Cranberry Lake)
Flora (Atherton)
George (Cranberry Lake)
Hazel (Cranberry Lake)

Beyerlein
Arnold (Edwards)
Bill (Edwards)
Diane (Edwards)
Judy (Edwards)
Kathy (Edwards)
Sandy (Edwards)

Bixby
Bell (Dale)
Herb (Dale)

Black
Don (Eastside)
Henry (Evergreen)
Joe (Evergreen)
Linda (Eastside)
Nancy (Eastside)
Sue (Eastside)

Blair
Addie (Evergreen)
Edward (Evergreen)
Gerald (Evergreen)
Harry (Evergreen)
Henry (Evergreen)
Joe (Evergreen)
Josie (Evergreen)
Margaret (Evergreen)
Merrill (Evergreen)
Virgil (Evergreen)

Blakely
Elna (Edwards)

Blane
Harry (Evergreen)

Boddy
Anna (Evergreen)
Charles (Dale, Evergreen)
Inez (Dale)
Myrtle (Dale)
Nina (Dale)
Robert (Dale, Evergreen)
Violet (Dale)

FAMILY NAME INDEX Continued

Boerner
Ernie (Dale)
Pearl (Dale)

Bohley
Anna (Evergreen)
Bertha (Evergreen)
Vernia (Evergreen)
Wilbert (Evergreen)

Bohlinger
Keith (Eastside)
Melvin (Eastside)
Verl (Eastside)

Bohnard
Beulah (Edwards)
Frank (Edwards)
Genevieve (Edwards)
Joe (Cook)
Josephine (Cook)
Lucille (Edwards)
Monroe (Edwards)
Rose (Cook)
Rosena (Edwards)

Boreland
Anna (Dale)
Inez (Dale)
Lottie (Dale)

Boun
Roy (Atherton)

Bowditch
Danny (Edwards)
Donald (Edwards)
Marilyn (Edwards, Erb)

Bowman
Earl (Atherton)
Mable (Atherton)

Mary Sue (Atherton)
Ola (Atherton)
Ralph (Atherton)
Ray (Atherton)

Bowsher
Don (Erb)

Earl (Edwards, Erb)
Joe (Erb)

Bradley
Harold (Eastside)
Kenneth (Eastside)

Bray
George (Cook, Erb)
Jack (Cook, Erb)

Brewer
Arthur (Erb)
Beatrice (Erb)
Diane (Eastside)
Floyd (Erb)
Hazel (Erb)
Joe (Erb)
Kenneth (Erb)
Polly (Erb)

Brick
Clarence (Campbell Corners)
Clyde (Campbell Corners)
Diane (Campbell Corners)
Dorothy (Campbell Corners)
Gerald (Campbell Corners)
Harold (Campbell Corners)
Judy (Campbell Corners)
Lizzie (Campbell Corners)
Lucille (Campbell Corners)
Luella (Campbell Corners)
Marie (Campbell Corners)
Mike (Campbell Corners)
Nancy (Campbell Corners)
Nyla (Campbell Corners)
Willie (Campbell Corners)

Brindley
Albert (Campbell Corners)
Bob (Cook)
Charles (Eastside)
David (Campbell Corners)
Delores (Cook)
Donna (Cook)
Frank (Campbell Corners)
Fred (Campbell Corners)
George (Campbell Corners)
Harold (Eastside)
Keith (Cook)
Larry (Cook)
Loretta (Cook)

Loren Jr. (Cook)
Mable (Campbell Corners)
Margaret (Cook)
Raymond (Cook)
Wanda (Cook)
William (Campbell Corners)

Brown
Eddie (Cook)
Jinnie (Cook)
Laura (Bell)

Broberg
Elaine (Eastside)

Brownley
Clyde (Edwards)
Cyril (Edwards)
Lester (Edwards)
Mildred (Edwards)

Buck
Clarence (Dale)

Buckel
Bob (Erb, Edwards)
Ed (Erb, Edwards)
Russell (Edwards, Erb)

Buckingham
Bonnie (East Side)
Bobby (Eastside)
Clyde (Eastside)
Ellis (Eastside)
Floyd (Eastside)
Janice (Eastside)
John (Eastside)
Lyle (Eastside)

Buhlman
Gerald (Cook)

Bunting
Raymond (Cook)
Roland (Cook)

FAMILY NAME INDEX Continued

Terry (Cook)

Burch
Dorothea (Bush Lake)
Stella (Bush Lake)

Burgher
Clarence (Erb)
Lois (Erb)
Lyle (Erb)
Ralph (Erb)
Richard (Erb)

Burt
Bill (Edwards)
Gladys (Edwards)
Helen (Edwards)
John (Edwards)
Irwin (Edwards)
Margaret (Edwards)
William (Edwards)

Busenbark
Florence (Busenbark)
James (Busenbark)
Leera (Busenbark)
Margaret (Busenbark)

Buyea
Grace (Edwards)

Byce
Arlene (Deckerville)
Vivian (Deckerville)

Campbell
Harry (Campbell Corners)
Hubert (Dale)
Courtland (Dale)

Carpenter
Grace (Edwards)
Mame (Edwards)

Carr
Lynn (Eastside)

Carrington

DeWitt (Dale)

Carscallen
Hildreth (Campbell Corners)
Irene (Campbell Corners)

Cascadden
Allen (Cook)
Althea (Cook)
Bill (Cook)
Debbie (Campbell Corners)
Judy (Cook)
Marvin (Campbell Corners)
Mary (Campbell Corners)

Caverly
Calvin (Caverly)
Emery (Caverly)
Lawrence (Caverly)
Warren (Caverly)

Chambers
Gloria (Cook)
Lois (Cook)
Lyle (Cook)

Chapman
Bob (Edwards)
David (Edwards)
Elsie (Edwards)
Marjorie (Edwards)
Peggy (Edwards)
Phyllis (Erb, Edwards)
Ruby (Edwards)

Chase
Charles (Campbell Corners)
Leonard (Evergreen)
Veda (Evergreen)
Verba (Evergreen)

Chatterson
Bill (Edwards)

Cheney
Clarence (Dale)

Christ
Sharon (Cook)

Clark
Bert (Dale)
Margaret (Cook)
Patricia (Cook)

Clayton
Arzel (Edwards)
Billy (Edwards)
Carl (Edwards)
Chuck (Erb)
Davis (Eastside)
Doris (Edwards)
Elton (Edwards, Erb)
Gordon (Edwards)
Grace (Edwards)
Helen (Edwards)
Jack (Erb)
James (Edwards)
Jerry (Eastside)
Margaret (Edwards)
Paul (Edwards, Erb)
Peter (Edwards)
Russell (Edwards)
Sadie (Edwards)
Tom (Erb)

Cody
Edward (Campbell Corners)

Cohoon
Claud (Edwards)

Combs
Lorraine (Cook)

Conley
Clarence (Dale)

Conrad
Nancy (Evergreen)

Cook
Alvin (Cook)
Ann (Cook)
Anna (Cook)
Arnold (Cook)
Avis (Dale)
Betty (Cook)
Billy (Cook)
Czar (Damon)
Ella (Cook)
Fred (Cook)
Greg (Cook)
Harold (Eastside)
Ida (Cook)
Janice (Cook)

FAMILY NAME INDEX Continued

Leonard (Cook)
Mary (Dale)
Mayme (Dale)
Myra (Damon)
Mona (Cook)
Robert (Cook)
Shirley (Cook)
Stella (Cook)
Tammy (Cook)
Willie (Cook)

Cool
Charlie (Campbell Corners)
Doris (Cook)
Eldon (Campbell Corners)
Eva (Campbell Corners)

Cooley
Hazen (Eastside)

Cooper
Bennie (Edwards)
Edgar (Edwards)
Eva (Edwards)
Floyd (Edwards)
Lawson (Edwards)

Copeland
Charlotte (Atherton)
Duane (Atherton)
Florene (Atherton)

Cornell
Leon (Bell)
Mervin (Bell)
Patricia (Bell)

Cornman
Russell (Dale)

Corwin
Marie (Dale)

Cross
Ernest (Campbell Corners)

Maurice (East Side)

Crow
Edith (Eastside)

Evan (Eastside)
Junior (Eastside)
Nina (Erb)

Cruickshank
Billy (Edwards)
Clair (Edwards)
Edna (Edwards)
Fred (Edwards)
Gordon (Edwards)
Jim (Edwards)
Keith (Edwards)
Leland (Edwards)
Lula (Edwards)
Roy (Edwards)

Cummings
Carol (Eastside)
John (Bush Lake)
Lynn (Eastside)
Maxine (Eastside)
Robert (Bush Lake)
Shirley (Eastside)

Curry
Donley (Atherton)
Margaret (Atherton)

Curtis
Carl (Erb)
Clayton (Erb)
David (Erb)
Dorothy (Erb)
George (Erb)
Glen Jr. (Erb)
Joe (Cook)
Lee (Erb)
Leith (Cook, Erb)
Linda (Cook)
Mary (Erb)
Mike (Cook)
Robert (Cook)
Virgil (Erb)

Dahl
William (Eastside)

Daniels
Geraldine (Beechwood)

Darling
Elizabeth (Edwards)
Iva (Edwards)

Vivian (Erb)

David
Arthur (Atherton)
Bernice (Atherton)
Byron (Atherton)
Chester (Atherton)
Daniel (Atherton)
DellaMae (Atherton)
Dewey (Atherton)
Doyle (Atherton)
Helen (Atherton)
Janice (Atherton)
Louis (Atherton)
Mae (Atherton)
Velma (Atherton)

Davis
Warren (Bell)

Daymon
Earl Jr. (Eastside)
Ivan (Eastside)

Decker
Angie (Edwards)
Bruce (Edwards)
Clair (Edwards)
Elmer (Edwards)
Ethel (Edwards)
Flossie (Edwards)
Gertrude (Edwards)
Glen (Edwards)
Goldie (Edwards)
Irene (Edwards)
Lucille (Edwards)
Mamie (Edwards)
Oscar (Edwards)
Walter (Edwards)

DeClute
Ida (Edwards)

Diehl
Betty (Caverly)

Denio
Alice (Campbell Corners)
Charles (Campbell Corners)

FAMILY NAME INDEX Continued

Denman
David (Campbell Corners)
Gaynol (Campbell Corners)
Sonya (Campbell Corners)

Dennison
Arthur (Campbell Corners)
Bertha (Campbell Corners)

Detzler
Bill (Eastside)
Sue (Eastside)

Diamond
Lottie (Damon)

Diebold
George (Cook)
Maude (Cook)
Pena (Cook)

Dill
Fred (Campbell Corners)
Todd (Campbell Corners)

Dishaw
Ben (Campbell Corners)
Bertha (Campbell Corners)
Cliffie (Campbell Corners)
Joseph (Campbell Corners)
Louis (Campbell Corners)
Paul (Campbell Corners)
Willie (Campbell Corners)

Dobler
Arthur (Cranberry Lake)
Billy (Cranberry Lake)
Dorothy (Cranberry Lake)

Dodds
Elmer (Atherton)
Eugene (Atherton)
Gladys (Atherton)
Grace (Atherton)
Harrison (Atherton)
Mable (Atherton)
Marion (Atherton)
Thelma (Atherton)

Doer
Chuck (Edwards)

Dolph
Bill (Evergreen)

Doron
Beatrice (Eastside)
Elinor (Eastside)
Isadore (Eastside)
Louis (Eastside)
Mary (Eastside)
Olive (Eastside)
Patience (Eastside)

Down
Mary (Eastside)

Drumm
Chuck (Eastside)

Drummond
Florence (Damon)

Dunlap
Harold (Eastside)
Juanita (Eastside)
Levere (Eastside)
Lucille (Eastside)
Quincy (Eastside)

Dunn
Bonnie (Edwards)
Carla (Edwards)
Cecil (Edwards)
Dick (Edwards)
Don (Edwards)
Doris (Edwards)
Judy (Edwards)
Karl (Edwards, Erb)
Kent (Edwards)
Kurt (Edwards)
Leonard (Edwards)

Durfee
Carl (Dale)
Charlene (Cook)
Harry (Cook)
Neil (Cook)
Sharon (Cook)
Shelly (Cook)

Duvekott
Edna (Bell)
Jennie (Dale)
Mattie (Dale)

Eadey
Gladys (Dale)
Hazel (Dale)

Earlie
Nora (Cranberry Lake)

Eastman
Betty (Atherton)
Eva (Atherton)
Frances (Atherton)
George (Atherton)
Howard (Atherton)
Iva (Atherton)
Jack (Atherton)
Leon (Atherton)
Neva (Atherton)
Raymond (Atherton)
Sally (Atherton)

Edmonds
Edwin (Dale)

Egan
Caroline (Cook)
Genevieve (Cook)
Mildred (Cook)

Ehinger
August (Edwards)
Betty (Cook)
Darrel (Edwards)
Debbie (Edwards)
Ronald (Edwards)
Tony (Edwards)
William Jr. (Cook)

Eineder
Nina (Erb)

Ellis
A. Jay (Edwards)
Emma (Eastside)
John (Eastside)

Emerson
Aleatha (Dale)
Alma (Dale)
Beatrice (Dale)
Bulah (Dale)
Ila (Dale)
Imogene (Dale)

Family Index Continued

Iris (Dale)
Juliaetta (Dale)
Thomas (Dale)
Waldo (Dale)

Engman
Emil (Cook)

Erb
Bill (Erb)

Evans
Gail (Cook)
Janet (Cook)
Karen (Cook)
Kirk (Cook)

Everitt
Evelyn (Erb, Evergreen)

Evilsizer
April (Edwards)
Dale (Edwards)
Don (Edwards)
Phyllis (Edwards)

Ewing
Caroline (Cook)
Clarence (Cook)
Clayton (Cook)

Exelby
Cindy (Cook)

Fahrner
Lloyd (Eastside)

Farro
Bill (Cranberry Lake)
Irene (Cranberry Lake)

Fayette
Gracie (Dale)
Lydia (Dale)
Mary (Dale)

Fell
Carrie (Cook)
Louise (Cook)

Ferguson
Brent (Eastside)
Joni (Campbell Corners)
Joyce (Eastside, Campbell Corners)
Ralph (Edwards)

Finerty
Clarence (Campbell Corners)
Edward (Campbell Corners)
George (Campbell Corners)
James (Campbell Corners)
John (Campbell Corners)
Katie (Cook)
Mamie (Campbell Corners)
Patrick (Campbell Corners)

Finnerty
Abbie (Cook)
Blanche (Cook)
Etta (Cook)
Maude (Cook)

Fisher
Austin (Campbell Corners)
Betty (East Side)
Brayton (Campbell Corners)
Eulalia (Eastside)
Jack (Eastside)
Nora (Eastside)
Robert (Eastside)

Flint
Muriel (Edwards)

Folsom
Charles (Eastside)

FitzGerald
Burton (Campbell Corners)
Clyde (Campbell Corners)
James (Campbell Corners)
Rola (Campbell Corners)

Flory
June (Edwards)

Fornwall
Emerson (Campbell Corners)
James (Campbell Corners)
Margaret (Campbell Corners)
Myrtle (Campbell Corners)

Fournier
Clarence (Edwards)

Eileen (Edwards, Erb)
Gary (Campbell Corners)
Georgina (Edwards, Erb)
Gerald (Edwards)
Greg (Edwards)
Idabel (Edwards)
Junior (Edwards, Erb)
Lillie (Edwards)
Napoleon (Edwards)
Randy (Campbell Corners)
Sandy (Campbell Corners)
Teresa (Edwards)
Theodore (Edwards, Erb)

Fox
Henry (Deckerville)
Lela (Deckerville)
Manley (Deckerville)
Sharrow (Deckerville)
Sydney (Deckerville)
Vera (Deckerville)
Virginia (Deckerville)

Franks
Vernon (Dale)

Freed
Florence (Campbell Corners)
Jessie (Campbell Corners)
Lizzie (Campbell Corners)
Maria (Campbell Corners)
Maudie (Campbell Corners)
Oliver (Campbell Corners)
Willie (Campbell Corners)

Freeman
Bobby (Erb)

French
Lizzie (Campbell Corners)

Fritz
Ada (Evergreen)
Joan (Bell)
John (Bell)
Lillian (Bell)
Mina (Bell)
Stephen (Bell)

Fry
Arthur (Eastside)

Family Index Continued

Fuller
Mamie (Edwards)

Galbraith
Helen (Edwards)
Wesley (Edwards)

Gallagher
Angeline (Eastside)
Art (Eastside)
Danny (Eastside)
Gary (Eastside)
James (Eastside)
Joe (Eastside)
Lawrence (Eastside)
Linda (Eastside)
Marie (Eastside)
Marjorie (Eastside)
Pat (Eastside)
Ruth (Eastside)
Thomas (Eastside)
Wilson (Eastside)

Gambler
Laverne (Eastside)

Gannon
Roy (Edwards)

Garish
Rose (Cranberry Lake)

Gehl
John (Cook)
Leo (Cook)
Leon (Cook, Cranberry Lake)
Richard (Cook)

Gerber
Amos (Edwards)
Daniel (Edwards)
David (Edwards)
Elizabeth (Edwards)
Eva (Cook)
Moses (Edwards)
Pete (Edwards)
Soloman (Edwards)

Gibson
Esma (Edwards)
George (Cranberry Lake)
Mary (Cranberry Lake)
Stella (Cranberry Lake)
Winona (Cranberry Lake)

Gildner
Alex (Edwards)
Catherine (Edwards)
Cecil (Edwards)
Clarence (Edwards)
David (Edwards)
Doug (Edwards)
Herbie (Edwards)
Hilda (Edwards)
Jeanette (Edwards)
John (Edwards)
Lucinda (Edwards)
Lucy (Edwards)
Marjorie (Edwards)
Mary (Edwards)
Roy (Edwards)
Valentine (Edwards)

Goatbe
Arthur (Atherton)
Georgia (Atherton)
Grace (Bush Lake)
Joyce (Bush Lake)
June (Bush Lake)
Norma (Atherton)

Good
Ada (Atherton)
Barbara (Atherton)
Billy (Atherton)
Bobby (Atherton)
Geneane (Atherton)
Geraldine (Atherton)
Henry (Atherton)
Leroy (Atherton)
Mildred (Atherton)
Nancy (Atherton)
Orland (Atherton)
Orville (Atherton)
Rosemary (Atherton)
Sally (Atherton)
Sonny (Atherton)
Wilbur (Atherton)

Graber
Leo (Dale)

Gray
Brian (Campbell Corners)
Louann (Eastside)
Michael (Campbell Corners)

Green
Alvena (Campbell Corners)
Beatrice (Erb)
Byron (Edwards)
Chloe (Edwards)
Eugene (Campbell Corners)
Frank (Erb)
Gertrude (Edwards)
Irene (Edwards)
Joe (Edwards)
LaVerne (Campbell Corners)
Melva (Erb)
Rose Marie (Erb)
Tryrus (Erb)
Vern (Erb)
Virginia (Erb)

Greer
Karen (Cook)
Larry (Cook)
Tim (Cook)

Grenier
Diane (Eastside)

Grezeszak
Albert (Eastside)

Griffin
Erma (Eastside)

Griffith
Sadie (Edwards)

Grossman
Albert (Campbell Corners)
Clyde (Campbell Corners)
Johnnie (Campbell Corners)
Philip (Campbell Corners)

Grow
Marion (Eastside)

Gruber
Hazel (Campbell Corners)

Gussman
Hattie (Evergreen)
Henry (Evergreen)
Paul (Evergreen)
Walter (Evergreen)

Family Index Continued

Hacht
Ada (Campbell Corners)
Alma (Campbell Corners)
AnnaMae (Campbell Corners)
Charlie (Campbell Corners)
Edith (Campbell Corners)
Florence (Campbell Corners)
Frances (Campbell Corners)
Fred (Campbell Corners)
Greg (Edwards)
James (Campbell Corners)
Katherine (Campbell Corners)
Maggie (Campbell Corners)

Hagerman
Oscar (Damon)

Hall
Claude (Bell)

Hamilton
Bud (Eastside)
Gladys (Edwards)
Gordon (Edwards)
Hazel (Edwards)
Irene (Edwards)
Lorn (Edwards)
Lucille (Edwards)
Lynn (Edwards)
Mable (Edwards)
Nauman (Edwards)
Orthella (Edwards)
Orville (Edwards)
Rhonda (Edwards)
Ruby (Edwards)
Sheri (Eastside)

Hanks
Bruce (Erb)
Nancy (Erb)

Hanson
Elsie (Erb)
Gene (Erb)
Geoge (Erb)
Jane (Erb)

Harbell
William (Damon)

Harrington
Milford (Bell)
Thelma (Bell)

Harris
Flynt (Evergreen)

Harshman
Doug (Campbell Corners)
Hubert (Campbell Corners)
Sharon (Campbell Corners)
Todd (Campbell Corners)

Hart
Grace (Eastside)
James (Campbell Corners)
Juanita (Eastside)
John (Eastside)
Leona (Eastside)
Mable (Campbell Corners)
Malvin (Campbell Corners)
Opal (Eastside)
Wilbur (Campbell Corners)

Hawley
Acel (Bell)
Agnes (Dale)
Arlene (Bell)
Clinton (Dale)
Donald (Bell)
Elaine (Dell)
Joan (Bell)
John (Dale)
Norman (Dale)
Sammy (Bell)
William (Bell)

Headley
Jessica (Campbell Corners)
Mike (Campbell Corners)

Hendricks
Della (Campbell Corners)
Henry (Campbell Corners)

Hennen
Bernice (Eastside)

Cecil (Eastside)
Dorothy (Eastside)
Gladys (Eastside)
Hilda (Eastside)
Joan (Eastside)
Lois (Eastside)
Marjorie (Eastside)
Mark (Eastside)
Maureen (Eastside)
Maurice (Eastside)
Vera (Eastside)

Hepner
Gale (Edwards)
Gladys (Edwards)
Leo (Edwards)

Herlick
Arlene (Campbell Corners)
Vivian (Campbell Corners)

Hicks
Eddie (Dale)

Higgens
Margarete (Cook)
Vera (Cook)

Hill
Pearl (Edwards)

Hiltz
Celia (Bell)
Effie (Bell)
Esther (Bell)
Ethel (Bell)
Harry (Bell)
Russell (Bell)

Hodgson
Frankie (Campbell Corners)

Holderied
Joe (Campbell Corners)
Mike (Campbell Corners)
Philip (Campbell Corners)

Hollowell
Elsie (Edwards)

Family Index Continued

Holshoe
  Agnes (Atherton)
  Alice (Atherton)
  Dick (Atherton)
  Donald (Atherton)
  Frank (Atherton)
  Ivadell (Atherton)
  Jerry (Atherton)
  Noreen (Atherton)
  Victor (Atherton)

Hook
  Carleen (Atherton)
  Renal (Atherton)

Hooper
  Juanita (Bell)

Horning
  Leighton (Atherton)
  Lotamae (Atherton)
  Marjorie (Atherton)
  Raymond (Atherton)
  Ruth (Atherton)

Hostetler
  Ezra (Atherton)

Houck
  Mildred (Bell)
  Carolyn (Atherton)
  Earl (Atherton)
  Edward (Atherton)
  Ezra (Atherton)
  Hazel (Atherton)
  Marcia (Atherton)

Housten
  Anna (Bell)

Hoyer
  Dennis (Cook)
  Dick (Cook)

Husted
  Ailene (Eastside)
  Betty (Eastside)
  Chuck (Eastside)
  Ester (Eastside)
  Gladys (Eastside)
  Helen (Eastside)
  Margaret (Eastside)
  Russell (Eastside)

Illig
  Adolph (Erb)
  Alfred (Erb)
  Althea (Cook, Edwards)
  Ambrose (Erb)
  Annamae (Edwards)
  Edward (Edwards)
  Floyd (Erb)
  Gary (Cook, Edwards)
  Genevieve (Erb)
  Georgina (Erb)
  Helen (Erb)
  Herman (Erb)
  Irene (Erb)
  James (Erb)
  Larry (Cook, Edwards)
  Leo (Erb)
  Leona (Erb)
  Linda (Cook, Edwards)
  Marsha (Cook, Edwards)
  Norman (Erb)
  Sherman (Erb)
  Tony (Erb)

Ingman
  Betty (Cook)

Ingram
  Clara (Dale)
  Hamilton (Dale)
  Ida (Dale)
  Laura (Dale)
  Orvin (Dale)
  Sarah (Dale)
  Truman (Dale)

Inman
  George (Beechwood)
  Hazel (Beechwood)
  Leon (Beechwood)
  Neil (Beechwood)

Jameson
  Joyce (Campbell Corners)

Jantzi
  Anna (Cook)
  Mary (Cook)

Jardin
  Lyman (Busenbark)
  Mernie (Busenbark)

Joye
  Jerry (Atherton)
  Judy (Atherton)

Kaiser
  Floyd (Edwards)

Kalmbach
  Margaret (Deckerville)

Kartis
  Francis (Cook)

Kauffman
  Adeline (Cook)
  Alvin (Cook)
  Barbara (Cook)
  Fannie (Cook)
  Floyd (Cook)
  Henry (Cook)
  Maud (Cook)

Kelsey
  Dan (Edwards)
  Delores (Edwards)
  Floyd (Erb, Edwards)
  Geraldine (Edwards)
  Leon (Edwards)

Kennedy
  Charley (Cook)
  Doris (Cranberry Lake)
  Ferman (Cook)

King
  Bernice (Edwards)
  Bob (Edwards)
  Donald (Edwards)
  Jack (Edwards)
  Mary (Cook)
  Orie (Edwards)
  Rozella (Cook)

Kinsey
  Alma (Dale)
  Lena (Dale)
  Viola (Dale)

Family Index Continued

Kish
  Helen (Cranberry Lake)
  Mary (Cranberry Lake)

Klann
  Tyrus (Erb)

Klemmer
  Kurt (Eastside)

Klug
  Fred (Edwards)
  Steve (Edwards)
  Terry (Edwards)

Knepfler
  Carl (Erb)
  Marie (Erb)

Knepler
  Anna (Cook)
  Francis (Cook)
  Mike (Cook)

Kohn
  Cearil (Evergreen)
  Clarence (Evergreen)

Kroll
  Nellie (Eastside)

Krug
  Willie (Cook)

Krugh
  Emma (Campbell Corners, Evergreen)
  George (Evergreen)

Kuhn
  Billy (Cook)
  Cora (Cook)
  David (Cook)
  Debra (Cook)
  Hursel (Cook)
  Mary (Cook)
  Mona (Cook)

Laberge
  Fred (Dale)
  Rocky (Dale)

Lafountain
  Ellen (Cook)
  Keith (Cook)
  Mary (Cook)

Lalonde
  Edith (Dale)
  George (Dale)
  Joseph (Dale)
  Levi (Dale)
  Viola (Dale)

Lang
  Albert (Eastside)
  Clara (Eastside)
  Edmund (Eastside)
  Julia (Eastside)
  Junior (Eastside)
  Mary (Eastside)
  Rosa (Eastside)
  Walt (Eastside)

Langley
  Ethel (Bell)

Lantern
  Mike (Edwards)

Lawrence
  Annabell (Bell)
  Charlie (Bell)
  Elizabeth (Bell)
  Fred (Bell)
  Harry (Bell)
  Mable (Bell)

Leathorn
  Velma (Dale)

Leckrone
  Samuel (Atherton)

Lehman
  Dale (Cook)
  Jack (Cook)
  Jerry (Cook)
  Larry (Cook)
  Mike (Cook)
  Phyllis (Cook)

Leonard
  Delbert (Campbell Corners)

Lester
  Donald (Cook)
  Julie (Cook)

Lewis
  Fannie (Dale)
  Lera (Busenbark)
  Mary (Dale)
  Nita (Busenbark)

Link
  Fred (Cook)
  George (Cook)
  Hattie (Cook)
  Martha (Cook)

Little
  Della (Campbell Corners)
  Emma (Campbell Corners)
  Ernie (Edwards)
  Helen (Campbell Corners)
  Herb (Edwards)
  Jimmie (Campbell Corners)
  Mike (Edwards)
  Tim (Edwards)

Livingood
  Beatrice (Eastside)
  Bernice (Eastside)

Lockwood
  Edith (Dale)
  George (Dale)
  Roy (Dale)

Lomason
  Ella (Damon)
  Grover (Damon)
  Joseph (Damon)
  Julia (Damon)

Loney
  Mary (Erb)

Family Index Continued

Loomis
Clarissa (Bell)
Darwin (Bell)
Ellen (Bell)

Loop
Fred (Edwards)

Lovell
Alice (Campbell Corners)
Kathleen (Campbell Corners)
Norman (Campbell Corners)
Russell (Campbell Corners)
Ruth (Campbell Corners)

Lucas
Jeff (Eastside)

Mackey
Jay (Cook, Edwards)
J. D. (Edwards)
Linda (Edwards)
Sue (Edwards)

Mackie
Hue (Campbell Corners)
Richard (Campbell Corners)
Teddy (Campbell Corners)

Madden
Beatrice (Edwards)
Florence (Edwards)

Mailloux
Rosa (Dale)
Virgie (Dale)

Mallach
Gwendolyn (Bush Lake)

Mannore
Ollie (Deckerville)

Marion
Berneatta (Dale)
Beulah (Dale)
Laurence (Dale)

Martin
Anita (Cook)
Bill (Cook)
Greg (Edwards)
Peggy (Cook)
Stanley (Cook)

Martindale
Alice (Atherton)
Aliene (Atherton)
Esther (Atherton)
Ilene (Atherton)
Tom (Atherton)
Viola (Atherton)

Mason
Bonnie (Atherton)
Donna (Atherton)
Fern (Atherton)
Harold (Atherton)
Mable (Atherton)
Sally (Atherton)
Steve (Atherton)
Twila (Atherton)
Wendel (Atherton)

Mathews
Neal (Evergreen)

Matthews
Bill (Deckerville)
Don (Deckerville)
George (Deckerville)
June (Deckerville)
Lawrence (Deckerville)
Oliver (Deckerville)
Reva (Deckerville)
Stanley (Dale)

Maxwell
Leon (Campbell Corners)
Randy (Campbell Corners)

May
Betty (Cranberry Lake)
Chester (Bush Lake)
Eunice (Bush Lake)
Loneta (Cranberry Lake)
Melvin (Cranberry Lake)
Nellie (Cranberry Lake)

Mayhew
Andy (Dale)
Betty (Beechwood, Dale)
Cherrian (Beechwood)
Del (Dale)
Reva (Dale)
Twila (Dale)
Wayne (Beechwood, Dale)

McAllister
Nanette (Eastside)

McCauley
Carl (Edwards)
Connie (Edwards)
Howard (Edwards)
Jennie (Edwards)
Keith (Edwards)
Maggie (Edwards)
Sam (Edwards)
Tom (Edwards)

McCracken
Glen (Dale)
Lucy (Dale)

McDonald
Alice (Cranberry Lake)
Clyde (Dale)
Harold (Cranberry Lake)
Jessie (Dale)

McGregor
Martha (Damon)
Merrian (Damon)
Merritt (Damon)
Robbie (Damon)

McIntyre
Verlyn (East Side)

McKellar
Agnes (Dale)
Alvin (Dale)
Donald (Dale)
Helen (Dale)
Mable (Dale)
Rachel ((Dale)

Family Index Continued

McKinnon
Jim (Campbell Corners)
Maryann (Campbell Corners)

McLean
Don (Eastside)
Gary (Eastside)

Meadows
Hattie (Evergreen)
Marion (Evergreen)
Nellie (Evergreen)
Ralph (Evergreen)

Meir
Gerald (Eastside)
Harvey (Atherton)
Irene (Eastside)
Lloyd (Eastside)
Mike (Atherton)
Paul (Atherton)
Philip Jr. (Eastside)
Rosemary (Atherton)
Tom (Atherton)

Meiser
David (Atherton)
Glen (Atherton)

Melrose
Doris (Cook)
Howard (Cook)
Phyllis (Cook)
Tom (Cook)

Mezzano
Dennis (Campbell Corners)

Mier
Ambrose (Campbell Corners)
Arthur (Campbell Corners)
Dorothy (Eastside)
Frank (Campbell Corners)
George (Campbell Corners)
Gertie (Campbell Corners)
Harold (Campbell Corners)
Kathy (Cook)
Larry (Cook)
Maggie (Campbell Corners)
Marie (Campbell Corners)
Ralph (Atherton)
Victor (Atherton)

Migan
Helen (Atherton)

Miles
Florence (Edwards)
Glen (Edwards)

Miller
Beverly (Atherton)
Douglass (Atherton)
Edna (Bell)
Francis (Cook)
Jim (Cook)
Jay (Dale)
Merral "Red" (Bell)
Mirl (Dale)
Nelda (Bell, Cook)
Norman (Atherton)
Paul (Cook)
Raymond (Atherton)
Roy (Bell)
Sandy (Eastside)
William (Cook)

Miracle
Bill (Bell)

Moats
Edith (Atherton)
Florence (Atherton)
Hazel (Atherton)
Lois (Atherton)
Vera (Atherton)
Zeta (Atherton)

Mogg
Mary Jane (Eastside)

Moore
Hazel (Dale)
Ida (Dale)
Jennie (Dale)
Martha (Dale)
Mary (Dale)

Moorehouse
Brenda (Atherton)
Don (Cranberry Lake)
Eddie (Atherton)
Jack (Bush Lake)
Kenneth (Atherton)
Millie (Atherton)
Nancy (Atherton)
Richard (Atherton)
Ronald (Atherton)

Morgan
Harold (Campbell Corners)

Morris
Burt (Eastside)
Daisy (Eastside)
Darrold Jr. (Cook)
Darrold Sr. (Cook)
Donald (Cook)
Eugene (Eastside)
Joyce (Eastside)
Tom (Eastside)

Most
Mabel (Cook)

Moyer
Donald (Evergreen)
Jean (Erb)

Munn
Diane (Campbell Corners)
Sharon (Campbell Corners)

Muntz
Alice (Cook)
Frank (Cook)
Ida (Cook)
Myrtle (Campbell Corners)

Mutch
Otis (Edwards)

Muzik
John (Cranberry Lake)
Julia (Cranberry Lake)
Mary (Cranberry Lake)
Mike (Cranberry Lake)

Family Index Continued

Myers
Helen (Atherton)
Jennie (Atherton)
Lena (Atherton)
Lula (Dale)
Marcella (Atherton)
Pearl (Atherton)

Nagy
Mary Jane (Edwards)

Nelson
Alice (Eastside)
Alma (Eastside)
Carol Jean (Eastside)
Irene (Eastside)
James (Eastside)
Karen (Eastside)
Lewis (Beechwood)
Louis (Eastside)
Richard (Eastside)
Robert (Eastside)
Seymour (Beechwood)

Neubecker
Abbie (Campbell Corners)
Bernice (Campbell Corners)
Chuck (Campbell Corners)
David (Eastside)
Emma (Campbell Corners)
Gladys (Campbell Corners)
Helen (Campbell Corners)
Jean (Campbell Corners)
Joan (Eastside)
Joyce (Campbell Corners)
Larry (Eastside)
LaVern (Campbell Corners)
Leo (Campbell Corners)
Lizzie (Campbell Corners)
Pat (Campbell Corners)
Ray (Campbell Corners)
Robert (Campbell Corners)
Ron (Campbell Corners, Eastside)
Roy (Campbell Corners)
Ruth Ann (Eastside)
Wanda (Campbell Corners)
Willie (Campbell Corners)

Neville
Nancy (Bell)
Rockford (Bell)

Newberry
Harold (Eastside)

Newcombe
Billy (Deckerville)
Carl (Deckerville)

Nichols
George (Bell)
Grace (Edwards)

Nixon
Harry (Campbell Corners)

Noel
Bernard (Cook)
Bobby (Edwards)
Charlene (Cook)
Charles (Edwards, Erb)
Dennis (Cook)
Margaret (Cook)
Mike (Cook)
Pau (Cook)
Tom (Edwards, Erb)
William (Edwards)

Noffsinger
Ann (Cook)
Jackie (Cook)
Jerry (Cook)
Jim (Cook)
Jo Ellen (Cook)
Judy (Cook)

Norris
Alla (Atherton)
Arlene (Atherton)
Dennis (Atherton)
Devere (Atherton)
Donley (Atherton)
Jennie (Atherton)
Kenneth (Atherton)
Leona (Atherton)
Lila (Atherton)
Maynard (Atherton)
Ora (Atherton)

Norton
Patricia (Campbell Corners)

O'Farrell
Earl (Dale)
Elmer (Dale)

Oliver
Adam (Edwards)
Alvin (Cook, Edwards)
Ernadine (Edwards)
Jerry (Erb)
Joan (Edwards)
Joyce (Edwards)
Max (Cook, Edwards)

Olson
Ethel (Atherton)
Eva (Atherton)
Gladys (Atherton)
Viola (Atherton)

Osborne
Junior (Edwards)

Ostrander
Augusta (Eastside)
Dallas (Eastside)
Delores (Eastside)
Donald (Eastside)
Edwin (Eastside)
Eva (Eastside)
Frank (Eastside)

Ouellett
Mary (Cook)

Oyster
Anna (Dale)
Beulah (Dale)
Carol (Campbell Corner, Eastside)
Earl (Dale)
Irvin (Dale)
Kenny (Campbell Corners)
Lloyd (Deckerville)
Mabelle (Dale)
Ralph (Dale)
Verna (Campbell Corners)
Virgil (Deckerville)

FAMILY NAME INDEX Continued

Palinski
Barbara (Erb, Edwards)

Palm
Philip (Cook)

Parkinson
Edwynna (Bell)
Janice (Bell)
Wayne (Bell)

Parliament
Brenda (Eastside)
Carol (Campbell Corners)
Clara (Campbell Corners)
Connie (Campbell Corners)
Delores (Campbell Corners)
Devere (Campbell Corners)
Doug (Campbell Corners)
Dwight (Campbell Corners, Eastside)
Kathy (Campbell Corners)
Leola (Campbell Corners)
Nettie (Campbell Corners)
Wesley (Campbell Corners)

Parr
Boyd (Bush Lake)

Parrish
Betty (Eastside)
Raymond (Eastside)
Ronald (Eastside)

Pausits
Frank (Cranberry Lake)
Joe (Cranberry Lake)
Raymond (Cranberry Lake)
Steve (Cranberry Lake)
Theresa (Cranberry Lake)

Pawson
Ida (Dale)
Jennie (Dale)
Mary (Dale)
Phebe (Dale)
Ray (Dale)

Payne
Alma (Atherton)
Elmer (Atherton)
George (Atherton)
Hazel (Atherton)
Mae (Atherton)

Peck
Bonnie (Eastside)

Pepper
Jeanette (Campbell Corners)

Perkins
Annabelle (Eastside)
Betty (Eastside)
Delbert (Eastside)
Dorothy (Eastside)
Helen (Eastside)
Kenneth (Eastside)
Ralph (Eastside)
Ray (Eastside)

Perry
Betty Gean (Eastside)
Carol (Eastside)
Earl Jr. (Eastside)
Mary Lou (Eastside)
Shirley Ann (Eastside)

Peters
Hazel (Evergreen)
Herman (Evergreen)
Viola (Evergreen)

Peterson
Beatrice (Atherton)
Blaine (Atherton)
Eldin (Atherton)
Emerson (Atherton)
Floyd (Atherton)
Henry (Atherton)
Linda (Atherton)
MaryAnn (Atherton)
Pearl (Atherton)
Rissie (Atherton)
Willard (Atherton)

Pettit
Alton (Bell)
Alvin (Bell)
Elaine (Bell)
Eveline (Bell)
Frone (Bell)
Wayne (Bell)

Pfeiffer
Harold (Edwards)
Harvey (Edwards)
Leonard (Edwards)
Norman (Edwards)

Philips
Jennie (Campbell Corners)
Peter (Campbell Corners)

Pinke
Margaret (Cranberry Lake)
Minnie (Cranberry Lake)

Poling
Frank (Eastside)
Mary Ida (Eastside)
Paul (Eastside)
Stacy (Eastside)
Tom (Eastside)

Pollington
Anna (Dale)
Viola (Erb)

Polmanteer
Almira (Bell)

Poplawski
Richard (Edwards)

Porter
Charley (Dale)
Jake (Dale)
William (Dale)
Willis (Dale)

FAMILY NAME INDEX Continued

Post
  Caroline (Erb)
  George (Erb)
  Jack (Erb)
  Leo (Erb)
  Milford (Erb)
  Morden (Erb)

Poyner
  Edward (Edwards)
  Linda (Edwards)

Preston
  Bernice (Campbell Corners)
  Ray (Campbell Corners, Eastside)

Prevo
  Joe (Edwards)
  Lester (Edwards)
  Shirley (Edwards)

Priest
  Lee (Eastside)

Przylubski
  Barbara (Edwards)

Purks
  Bennie (Bell)
  Deforest (Bell)
  Heighter (Bell)
  Merlin (Bell)

Quackenbush
  Althea (Damon)

Quick
  Janet (Campbell Corners)
  Jerry (Campbell Corners)
  Martha (Campbell Corners)
  Ronald (Campbell Corners)

Rank
  Martha (Dale)

Rankin
  Crystal (Dale)

Rau
  Bethal (Cook)
  Gerald (Edwards)
  Jeri (Edwards)
  Julie (Edwards)
  Keith (Cook)
  Robert (Cook)

Raymond
  Betty (Cook)
  Bonnie (Cook)
  Jimmy (Cook)

Reasner
  Raymond (Dale)

Reed
  David (Cook)
  Donald (Cook)
  Lucille (Dale)
  Mary (Cook)
  Ronald (Cook)

Reese
  Carl (Edwards)

Reetz
  Charles (Evergreen)
  Clarence (Evergreen)
  Doris Jean (Evergreen)
  Dwight (Evergreen)
  Edward (Campbell Corners, Evergreen)
  George (Evergreen)
  Gladys (Evergreen)
  Helen (Evergreen)
  Jack (Campbell Corners)
  Jane (Campbell Corners)
  Mabel (Evergreen)
  Margaret (Campbell Corners)

Regan
  Ama (Cook)
  Belle (Cook)
  Jennie (Cook)
  Ned (Cook)

Reilly
  Ella (Bell)

Reinhardt
  Alice (Eastside)
  Edwina (Eastside)
  Emma (Eastside)
  Eugene (Eastside)
  Margaret (Busenbark)

Remer
  Ella (Evergreen)
  Willie (Evergreen)

Resteiner
  John (Cook)
  Walter (Cook)

Rhines
  Butch (Edwards)
  Charles (Edwards)
  John (Edwards)
  Mona (Edwards)

Rich
  Doris (Busenbark)
  Jenny (Busenbark)
  Kenny (Busenbark)
  Oney (Busenbark)

Richardson
  Ben (Eastside)
  Keith (Eastside)
  Jack (Eastside)
  Theodore (Eastside)

Robinson
  Kathleen (Atherton)
  Shelia (East Side)

Roches
  Edwinna (Erb)
  Leo (Erb)
  Pat (Erb)

Rohl
  Fletcher (Campbell Corners)
  Mervyn (Campbell Corners)

Root
  Patricia (Campbell Corners)

FAMILY NAME INDEX Continued

Rose
Joseph (Edwards)

Rosebrugh
Allen (Campbell Corners)
Brenda (Campbell Corners)
Carl (Campbell Corners)
Earla (Campbell Corners)
Emma (Bell)
Frank (Bell)
John (Bell)
Judson (Campbell Corners)
Lucie (Campbell Corners)
Mark (Campbell Corners)
Reid (Campbell Corners)
Roxie (Bell)

Rowe
Dean (Atherton)
Joyce (Atherton)

Rowland
Floyd (Evergreen)

Ruegsegger
Doris (Erb, Edwards)
Katherine (Erb, Edwards)

Rundel
Joseph (Edwards)
Ona (Edwards)
Wesley (Edwards)

Runyan
Fred (Cranberry Lake)
Rosie (Cranberry Lake)
Wilbur (Cranberry Lake)

Ryan
Mickey (Atherton)

Safford
Annella (Cook)

Sage
Lizzie (Damon)

St. John
Flora (Edwards)
Grace (Edwards)
Karen (Campbell Corners)
Pat (Campbell Corners)

Schaffer

Frank ((Erb)
LeRoy (Erb)
Marion (Erb)
Patty (Erb)
Sandy (Erb)

Schalk
Charmane (Campbell Corners)
Joey (Campbell Corners)
Mary (Campbell Corners)
Norman (Campbell Corners)
Shirley (Campbell Corners)

Scheele
Bernard (Cook)
Doris (Cook)
Eddie (Cook)
Flora (Cook)
George (Cook)
Helen Jane (Cook)
Marjorie Ann (Cook)
Marlene (Cook)
Priscilla (Cook)
Ruth Ann (Cook)

Schliter
Bob (Edwards)
Connie (Edwards)

Schmidt
Murray (Erb)

Schmitt
Aleen (Campbell Corners)
Alice (Campbell Corners)
Betty (Campbell Corners)
Bob (Campbell Corners)
Dean (Campbell Corners)

Ethel (Campbell Corners)
Jake (Campbell Corners)
Jerry (Campbell Corners)
John (Campbell Corners)
Junior (Campbell Corners)
Marge (Campbell Corners)
Mary (Campbell Corners)
Murry (Erb)
Olith (Campbell Corners)
Toby (Campbell Corners)

Schneider
Doris (Evergreen)
Elmer (Evergreen)
Ernest (Evergreen)
Ervin (Evergreen)
Gerald (Evergreen)
John (Evergreen)
Mary Ann (Campbell Corners)
Ronald (Evergreen)

Schultz
Howard (Caverly)

Scott
Addie (Cook)
Cloie (Cook)
Johnny (Cook)
Larry (Cook)
Lorraine (Eastside)
Sharon (Cook)

Sedore
Dorothy (Eastside)
Hallie (Eastside)
Nora (Eastside)
Ralph (Eastside)

Selmes
Donna (Eastside)

Seltz
Vicky (Eastside)

FAMILY NAME INDEX Continued

Sergent
Ben (Edwards)
Gary (Edwards)
Jack (Edwards)
Jay (Edwards, Erb)
Jean (Edwards, Erb)
Jim (Edwards)
Joyce (Edwards, Erb)
Kathryn (Edwards)
Phyllis (Edwards)
Walter (Edwards, Erb)

Sharpe
Bert (Cook)
Joe (Cook)
Minnie (Cook)
Steve (Cook)

Shattuck
Blaine (Bell)
Maxine (Bell)

Sheil
Jean (Cook)

Sheldon
Ellen (Beechwood)
Forest (Beechwood)

Sheltrown
Buster (Erb)
Clyde (Erb)
Doreen (Erb)
Dorothy (Erb)
Eddie (Erb)
Erma (Erb)
Evelyne (Erb)
Jim (Erb)
Ida Bell (Erb)
Louise (Erb)
Myrtle (Erb)
Raymond (Erb)
Ray Jr. (Erb)

Shepherd
Amber (Eastside)

Sias
Miranda (Edwards)

Siegle
Edna (Eastside)
Elizabeth (Eastside)
Everitt (Eastside)
Mary (Eastside)

Simon
Irma (Cranberry Lake)
Olga (Cranberry Lake)

Simpson
Billy (Eastside)

Slater
Charlie (Campbell Corners)
Vera (Bell)

Sleeman
Barbara (Eastside)
Betty (Eastside)
Erma (Eastside)
Richard (Eastside)

Slosser
Joyce (Eastside)

Smaltz
Frank (Cook)

Smith
Cora (Dale)
Gertie (Dale)
Ethel (Campbell Corners)
Harold (Campbell Corners)
Jane (Campbell Corners)
John (Campbell Corners)

Snooks
Johnny (Atherton)
Mary Jane (Atherton)
Myrtle (Atherton)
Viola (Atherton)

Spafford
Mina (Dale)
Minnie (Dale)

Spahn
Audrey (Edward)
Donna (Edwards)
Leo (Edwards)

Spearman
Don (Bell)

Spencer
Cordia (Evergreen)
Dean (Erb)
Lelah (Evergreen)
Nellie (Evergreen)

Sperling
Bernard (Cook)
Linda (Cook)
Terry (Cook)

Spierling
Charlie (Evergreen)

Stamm
Eddie (Cook)
Jim (Cook)
Steven (Cook)

Stanlake
Frank (Campbell Corners)
Mae (Campbell Corners)
Oscar (Campbell Corners)

Steele
Elmer (Cranberry Lake)
Geraldine (Cranberry Lake)

Stephens
Samuel (Cranberry Lake)

Stevenson
Lowell (Cook)

Stinson
Bertie (Dale)
Jimmie (Dale)

FAMILY NAME INDEX Continued

Stone
 Bonnie (Atherton)
 Christina (Atherton)
 Clara (Edwards)
 Edward (Edwards)
 Eva (Atherton)
 Harold (Atherton)
 John (Edwards)
 Leah (Atherton)
 Lee (Edwards)
 Mary (Atherton)
 Robert (Atherton)

Stotler
 Louella (Bell)

Stringer
 Barb (Eastside)
 Jimmy (Eastside)
 Maggie (Edwards)

Strong
 Annie (Cook)
 Sherry (Cook)

Suggum
 Ada (Dale)

Sutherland
 Albert (Eastside)
 Carl (Eastside)
 Ernest (Eastside)
 Floyd (Eastside)
 Harold (Eastside)
 Inez (Eastside)
 Mary (Eastside)
 Mildred (Eastside)
 Roy (Eastside)

Sutton
 Cameron (Bell, Erb)
 Crandall (Erb, Edwards)
 Donna (Edwards, Erb)
 Milton (Erb)
 Ronald (Edwards, Erb)

Switzer
 Berdie (Atherton)
 Charlie (Atherton)
 Dean (Atherton)
 Dorothy (Atherton)
 Harold (Atherton)

Tabaca
 Eugene (Eastside)

Tabor
 Gene (Eastside)

Taft
 Erma (Cook)
 Terrance (Cook)

Talbot
 Abbie (Dale)
 Ada (Dale)
 Dora (Dale)
 Ida (Dale)
 Johnie (Dale)

Tank
 Beverly (Edwards)
 Clayton (Edwards)

Tanner
 Jay (Dale)

Taylor
 Charlotte (Caverly)
 Floyd (Eastside)
 George (Eastside)

Teeple
 Gladys (Dale)
 Lawrence (Dale)

Teeples
 Ellis (Beechwood)
 Gladys (Dale)
 J. R. (Beechwood)
 Laverne (Beechwood)
 Lawrence (Beechwood)
 Lewis (Beechwood)

Thayer
 Geo. (Dale)
 Jane (Dale)
 Myrtle (Dale)
 William (Dale)

Thompson
 Lois (Eastside)

Thorn
 Maryann (Atherton)
 Nelson (Atherton)

Thorne
 Alfred (Atherton)
 Viola (Atherton)
 William (Atherton)

Thornton
 Cecil (Evergreen)
 Iva (Evergreen)

Timlick
 Betty (Edwards)
 Lila (Edwards)

Thorp
 Bob (Campbell Corners)

Tolfree
 Marie (Edwards)

Toth
 Elizabeth (Cranberry Lake)
 Emil (Cranberry Lake)

Trout
 Beverly (Atherton)
 Debbie (Campbell Corners, Eastside)
 Diane (Eastside)
 Erma (Atherton)
 Kathy (Campbell Corners)
 Marvin (Atherton)
 Mike (Campbell Corners)
 Rita (Atherton)
 Russell (Campbell Corners)
 Verah (Atherton)

FAMILY NAME INDEX Continued

Tupper
Belle (Edwards)
Blanche (Edwards)
Robert (Edwards)

Turk
Anna (Campbell Corners)
Frances (Campbell Corners)
Lena (Campbell Corners)
Mary (Campbell Corners)

Turland
Jim (Bell)
Margaret (Bell)

Turley
Mary (Dale)
Elsie (Dale)
Grace (Dale)
Leeds (Dale)

Tuttle
Dorothy (Edwards)
DeWayne (Edwards, Erb)

Twiliger
May (Evergreen)

Utter
Almeda (Edwards)
Clara (Bell)
Oka (Edwards)
Sandra (Edwards)
Sharon (Edwards)

Valent
John (Cranberry Lake)

Valley
Abner (Eastside)
Donna (Eastside)
Mabel (Campbell Corners)
Mack (Campbell Corners)
Merritt (Campbell Corners)
Morris (Campbell Corners)
Norine (Eastside)
Ray (Evergreen)
Vivian (Eastside)

Vatter
Clarence (Cranberry Lake)

Vandenberg
Donna (Eastside)
Harold (Eastside)
Howard (Eastside)

Van Dyke
Elly Jo (Cook)

Van Martin
Adelbert (Damon)

Van Meer
Henry (Cranberry Lake)
Mary (Cranberry Lake)

VanWormer
Lucille (Atherton)

Vaughn
Amos (Evergreen)
Sarah (Evergreen)
Shirley (Evergreen)

Voss
Jan (Campbell Corners)

Wade
Clair (Edwards)
Duane (Edwards)
Helen (Edwards)
Howard (Edwards)
Margaret (Edwards)
Warren (Edwards)

Waite
Alice (Dale)

Walker
Delbert (Eastside)
Raymond (Cranberry Lake)
Wayne (Eastside)

Wallar
Dewey (Edwards)
Hazen (Edwards)

Walls
John (Edwards)
Max (Edwards)

Walter
Clyde Junior (Bush Lake)

Walters
Judy (Cook)
Louise (Cook)
Stanley (Edwards)

Wangler
Bernard (Eastside)
Dallas (Eastside)
Dave (Campbell Corners)
Gary (Campbell Corners)
Harold (Campbell Corners)
Helen (Eastside)
Jackelyn (Eastside)
Jane (Campbell Corners)
Jeff (Campbell Corners)
Jerry (Campbell Corners)
Marlene (Campbell Corners)
Mary (Eastside)
Mary Lou (Eastside)
Maxine (Campbell Corners)
Nedra (Campbell Corners)
Ronnie (Eastside)
Ronny (Campbell Corners)
Steve (Campbell Corners)
Terry (Campbell Corners)
Viola (Campbell Corners)
Willard (Campbell Corners)

Ware
Jesse (Dale)
Ray (Dale)
Lloyd (Dale)
Elsie (Dale)

Warren
Betty (Cook)
Robert (Cook)
Ruth Ann (Cook)
Sandra (Cook)

FAMILY NAME INDEX Continued

Werblo
 Joe (Cook)

Westwick
 Hazel (Erb)

Wheeler
 Pat (Evergreen)
 Paul (Evergreen)

Whipple
 Kenneth (Erb)
 Maxine (Erb)

White
 Edward (Erb)
 Evelyn (Erb)
 Fred (Erb)
 Marion (Deckerville)
 Mary (Erb)
 Russell (Deckerville)

Whitman
 Lena (Cook)
 Ross (Cook)

Wickert
 Edna (Cranberry Lake)
 Stella (Cranberry Lake)
 Wilma (Cranberry Lake)

Wilcox
 Lyle (Eastside)

Wilder
 Leslie (Dale)

Wilkenson
 Conover (Cook)
 Jay (Cook)
 Marjorie (Cook)
 Zora (Cook)

Wilkinson
 Eugene (Cranberry Lake)

Willett
 Dick (Cook)
 Linda (Cook)
 Martha (Cook)
 Nancy (Cook)
 Patricia (Cook)
 Ronald (Cook)
 Rosie (Cook)

Williams
 Alma (Edwards)
 Bernadene (Edwards)
 Boyd (Edwards)
 Catherine (Edwards)
 Charlotte (Edwards)
 Clarabelle (Edwards)
 Cora (Edwards)
 Donald (Edwards)
 Donna (Bush Lake)
 Faye (Edwards)
 Garnet (Eastside)
 Leota (Edwards)
 LeRoy (Eastside)
 Lucy (Edwards)
 Marvin (Bush Lake)
 Ray (East Side)
 Thelma (Edwards)
 Warren (Edwards)

Wilson
 Ella (Campbell Corners)
 Johnnie (Campbell Corners)
 Kathleen (Eastside)

Wiltse
 Alvin (Bell)
 Chester (Bell)
 Hazel (Bell)
 Minnie (Bell)

Wing
 Leslie (Campbell Corners)

Winter
 Clyde (Eastside)
 Henrietta (Eastside)
 Jack (Eastside)
 Marion (Eastside)
 Merceda (Eastside)
 Ned (Eastside)

Winters
 Alma (Campbell Corners)
 Andrew (Cook)
 Frank (Cook)
 Willie (Cook)

Wirges
 Harvey (Cook)
 Jacob (Cook)
 Mary (Cook)
 Rose (Cook)
 Tillie (Cook)

Withey
 Anna Belle (Bell)

Woodiwiss
 Iva (Campbell Corners)
 Johnnie (Campbell Corners)
 Nellie (Campbell Corners)
 Theodore (Campbell Corners)

Woodrow
 Eddie (Damon)
 Maud (Damon)
 May (Damon)

Woughter
 Daniel (Campbell Corners)
 Dave (Campbell Corners)
 Dennis (Campbell Corners)
 Gerald (Campbell Corners)
 Jim (Campbell Corners)
 Mark (Campbell Corners)

Wright
 William (Caverly)

Wyman
 Hattie (Atherton)
 Elaine (Atherton)

Yates
 Walter (Cranberry Lake)

Young
 Jeffery (Cook)
 Jessie (Cook)
 Jim (Cook)
 John (Cook)

FAMILY NAME INDEX Continued

Zahm
George (Eastside)
Raymond (Eastside)

Zaidl
Mike (Bush Lake)

Zettle
Bill (Cook)
David (Campbell Corners)
Diane (Cook)
Donald (Campbell Corners)
Greg (Campbell Corners)
Jerome (Campbell Corners)
John (Cook)
Magdaline (Cook)
Regina (Cook)
Rick (Cook)
Rozena (Cook)

Zsidy
Charles (Cranberry Lake)
Joe (Cranberry Lake)

Ziembo
Charles (Cook)
Julius (Cook)

Zimmerman
Eudoras (Dale)

Zink
Fred (Erb)
Junior (Erb)

Ogemaw County Genealogical & Historical Society

OGEMAW COUNTY HISTORICAL MUSEUM

The Ogemaw County Genealogical and Historical Society acquired the "Blumenthal House" in December, 2012 as a donation from Lavere Webster. The house is located on the corner of First and Wright Streets in West Branch.

Society members and volunteers plan to restore the house to its original charm and beauty and to open it as the Ogemaw County Historical Museum in 2016.

On-going preservation and maintenance of the building, as well as extensive archives of Ogemaw history and artifacts, remains the goal of the Society.

For further information, please contact the Ogemaw County Genealogical and Historical Society at Post Office Box 734, West Branch, Michigan 48661
Phone (989) 701-2525, email oghs1978@gmail.com on Facebook: Ogemaw County Historical Museum and at our webpage: https://www.ogemawcountyhistoricalsociety.com

Ogemaw County Genealogical & Historical Society

www.ingramcontent.com/pod-product-compliance
Lightning Source LLC
Chambersburg PA
CBHW081220170426
43198CB00017B/2669